THE FINE ART
of
NEEDLEPOINT

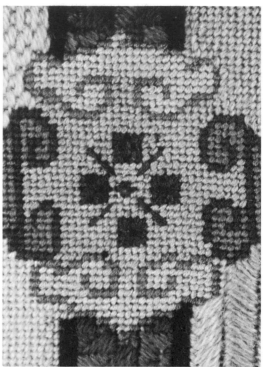

THE FINE ART
of
NEEDLEPOINT

MURIEL B. CROWELL

THOMAS Y. CROWELL COMPANY

NEW YORK   ESTABLISHED 1834

PHOTOGRAPHS BY RAY EGAN

DIAGRAMS BY DOLORES KLUGA

DESIGNED BY ABIGAIL MOSELEY

Manufactured in the United States of America

ISBN 0-690-29799-8

1 2 3 4 5 6 7 8 9 10

Library of Congress Cataloging in Publication Data

Crowell, Muriel B
    The fine art of needlepoint.

    1. Canvas embroidery.   I. Title.
TT778.C3C76 1973   746.4′4   73-9564
ISBN 0-690-29799-8

To my darling man,
whose unselfishness and patience
got him through this book.

My thanks to designers Darcy Beyer, Merrill Crowell, Leah Goodman, Sandra Kuntz, Linda Olsheim, Cecily Zerega and to consultants Sandra Casselano of Paternayan Bros. and Ruth Earle Brittan. A special gold star to my editor, Cynthia Vartan.

Foreword

This book is the perfect needlepoint book. Good for those of us who have been addicts for years and need new inspiration and for those about to become addicted to this happy pastime.

Dorothy Hammerstein

Contents

Introduction

Needlepoint stitches have personalities. Some march across the canvas like wooden soldiers; others pop out like polka dots; and still others lie flat as reeds. There are hundreds of different kinds. The sixty included in this book were chosen primarily for their ability to complement a design and to enhance the finished articles that feature them.

The most popular stitch and the workhorse of them all is the Tent stitch. In fact, some people think that needlepoint is nothing but this single slanting stitch, and they use it to the exclusion of all others. Certainly some of the most outstanding pieces in needlepoint art have been done in the Tent stitch, and it is obviously here to stay. But it is a pity not to know other stitches enough to be able to experiment with them and use them in conjunction with the Tent stitch. In order to do so, you need more than a description of various other stitches. You need to know where best to use them. It is for this reason that this book was written.

An illustration of one single stitch or even three or four worked in a cluster or row will not give an adequate picture of the effects that can be produced. Even in the embroiderer's dictionary, the sampler, where the examples of stitches are worked in adjoining shapes, the interesting potential of individual stitches does not show to advantage. They seem merely small swatches of fabric totally unrelated to each other. To make these stitches work for you and for each other as design elements, you must be able to visualize how they will look if worked in small areas, in large areas, or as background. You must know how they will look as an accent and in juxtaposition to other stitches. You must know what their texture will be and how they will wear. You must know their degree of

Stitches, Stitch Units,
and Patterns

In needlepoint, or canvas embroidery, all stitches are worked into the open mesh of a piece of canvas, unlike surface embroidery or crewel work where the stitches are worked on the surface of a piece of finished backing, such as linen or cotton.

The word *stitch* may refer to one in-and-out movement of needle and thread, or it may refer to several such movements covering from one to a dozen or more canvas intersections, forming layers like an orderly pile of jackstraws. Any variation from the basic needlepoint stitches are sometimes referred to as "ornamental stitches." The mechanics of

working these stitches are not difficult, particularly when one understands that all stitches in canvas embroidery are only worked vertically, horizontally, or diagonally. These three kinds of stitches going in various directions in different sequences, sizes, and layers form stitch units that are the building blocks of needlepoint and lend themselves to innumerable combinations.

They can make fascinating shapes, some as round and compact as little sunbursts, others as lacy and delicate as snowflakes. Some form diamonds, triangles, squares, or rectangles. Cross-stitches and uprights can glide along the

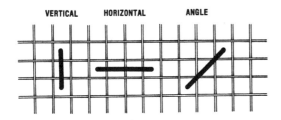

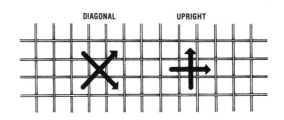

canvas making weaves and textures that are as rough as an English tweed or as smooth as a Florentine damask, depending upon the stitch formula. Outline stitches can swing around the edge of flowers like tinsel trimmings on a Christmas tree, while others simulate the feathers of a bird. Aside from these many shapes, forms and textures, these stitch units also may be repeated, side by side forming lovely fabric-like patterns.

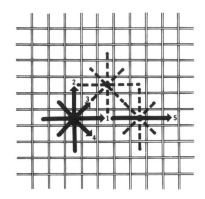

Needlepoint
Is a Decorator's Delight

Needlepoint is a hobby for those who care. A house becomes a home when there is a touch of oneself in it. We Americans have been busy making homes ever since the days of the first settlers and are still at it with as much verve and enthusiasm as we were generations ago. We have prided ourselves on the ability to create with our hands, and it has become an admirable quality that we cannot and do not want to overcome. Needlepoint is a personal art that helps us harness this creative urge, which is part of our heritage. To have a hobby that is relaxing and comforting and at the same time can produce a stunning accessory for a home is what keeps the fingers

flying. We all like to "keep busy." This characteristic may stem from our New England forebears who instilled into their children, particularly little girls, the ugly thought that if they didn't keep their fingers busy, worms would grow in them.

We are born decorators, and needlepoint is a decorator's delight. Many a room has been built around a piece of needlepoint. This is not only common to this country nor is it the result of present-day "do-it-yourself" programs. In eighteenth-century England, the Adam brothers, those talented interior innovators who brought bits of Greek temples into the home, were commissioned by the Earl of Coventry to build a room to complement a favorite Gobelin tapestry design that had been made into wall hangings and chair seats. It is hard for us to imagine constructing paneling, ceiling, moldings and furniture to go with a chair seat, but that was not an unusual request in that century when craftsmen and cabinet makers were to be found two or three to a village. In a less flamboyant way, there are still homeowners today who want to use a favorite painting, an heirloom bedspread, or a piece of needlepoint as a theme for a decorating scheme. And many a room has been highlighted by the addition of a piece of needlepoint on a footstool; many a dark corner brightened by a colorful pillow.

In the Middle Ages, rugs and wall hangings of canvas embroidery, or needlepoint, were used for warmth as well as decoration. In Elizabethan England, Mary Queen of Scots, during her eighteen years of imprisonment, became almost manic in her passion for needlepoint, and she made cushions, bell pulls, bed hangings, and chair covers to brighten the walls of her dismal fortress. She and her ladies spent many long hours devising new stitches. She presented some of her handiwork to her cousin Elizabeth perhaps in the hope that the sentimental phrases embroidered into her pieces might soften that harsh lady. Secret messages in code were also worked into her needlework and smuggled out to her friends. Elizabeth also was an ardent embroiderer. Her approach was less frantic, and she kept herself and her ladies supplied with "Pattern Books," which made an appearance about that time. These books were filled with designs, usually of flora and fauna motifs for the needleworker to copy, so any thoughts

that these Elizabethan court ladies sat in an orangerie, copying caterpillars from life, must be quickly dashed. When Elizabeth authorized contests, groups of them assembled daily to work on their embroidery, and the forerunner of the quilting bee was in full swing.

The early American colonists were less ardent about needlepoint because it took up too much of their limited supply of precious yarn, but as they prospered, so did the use of canvas embroidery and many decorative objects survive. Martha Washington needlepointed the seats for the dining-room chairs in her household.

The Victorian period produced thousands of musty-colored footstools covered in needlepoint. The Victorians also wore needlepoint. The ladies had their mantles or stoles done in heavy cotton thread, interspersed with an occasional bead for eye appeal, while the men had their canvas-embroidered vests.

During the days of the glitter and the gold, when the American railroad barons wanted to emulate the European manor houses and castles, needlepoint became a priceless decorative feature. These elaborate mansions required wall hangings in keeping with the period they represented. Original French antique wall hangings, worked in cross-stitches and the Tent stitch, were difficult to acquire since few had survived the Revolution. Skillful needlewomen were commissioned to design and reproduce magnificent works of a sophisticated motif similar to those found on the walls of those to the "manor born." We might say that needlepoint reached its zenith in the United States in the early 1900's during that period of affluence before World War I. But those days were short-lived, terminated by the war, and handworked "needlepoint tapestry" was replaced by the machine.

In the 1920's, needlepoint again became the rage. The Tent stitch was soon adorning everything but tents. As I look back, it seems as if I spent my childhood waiting in a needlework department for my mother, staring through the hot glass showcases at "traméd" canvases showing designs of pompadoured ladies reclining amidst a bower of bowknots and flowers. *Tramé* is an underlay of colored yarn running on the horizontal of the canvas forming the design and indicating the change of colors, and usually worked over in the Tent stitch or cross-stitch. The canvas was double-weave Penelope—an unfortunate faded khaki color—and the yarn, though in subtle colors, was heavy and lusterless. Many beautiful pieces of needlepoint, however, were produced from these imported canvases. Our linen closet bulged with canvases for chair seats, loveseats, and footstool covers being saved to work on a rainy day. It rained for eight chair seats, and we sat for our meals on cabbage roses on a dark brown background. The roses had been worked by some stranger in a far-off land. The backgrounds were done in the Continental stitch, the only popular stitch at the time. I don't know how much dark brown yarn my mother bought, but my children estimate three to four miles.

Today we are in the midst of a new needlepoint vogue. Needlepointers get a tremendous satisfaction out of selecting colors and choosing stitches for a design, even though they are unable to paint the original themselves. We have an Impressionist's palette of yarn colors to use, a choice of designs that encompasses every motif, and a variety of flexible stitches in which to express ourselves.

The needlepoint "kit" is here to stay for those who like to be told what to do. It is not an innovation; George Washington was wrapped up in one as early as the 1800's and can be seen in the same pose, in the same colors, in at least two of our museums today. The careful instructions and the prechoice of colors give security to the needlepoint novice, and kits have been responsible for leading many on to more ambitious projects and elaborate stitches.

Practically—that ugly New England word—needlepoint is indestructible and can outwear most fabrics. It has survived for hundreds of years. A piece was found in pretty fair shape in the tomb of an Egyptian king dating from the Middle Kingdom. During the 1800's, however, unnecessary precautions were often taken to preserve "fancy work." In Nantucket, in one of those fabulously restored houses, there is a cute little stool with the design off-center. This was purposely done, so that the user would not put his feet on the pattern. Less subtle measures are often taken today. Actually needlepoint is so rugged and so easily cleaned—even washed—that it is ridiculous to take such precautions.

The cry of many needlepointers after having completed two or three cushions is, What else can I make? It's true that the most successful and popular article made from needlepoint is a cushion; it is light to carry while working and attractive in any decor. But there are also a multitude of other lovely and useful items to be made. In fact, when one first sees the list, some may seem a little contrived. However, upon sorting them out and visualizing them worked in several different designs and a variety of stitches, they become quite intriguing.

The list includes belts, slippers, collars and cuffs, vests, cummerbunds, blazer pockets, skirts, purses, eyeglass cases, tote bags, briefcases, mail baskets, boxes, book covers, luggage, coat hangers, garment protectors, pins, buttons, tennis-racket covers, golf-club mitts, bicycle seats, binnacle covers, burgee colors, yachting chairs, seat belts, desk sets, portfolios, picture frames, coasters, bookends, paperweights, mirror frames, Christmas ornaments, chair seats, footstool covers, bench covers, cocktail-table and tray tops, lamp bases, firescreens, drapery valances, chair rails, doorstops, card-table tops, rugs, luggage racks, table mats, church appointments, pictures, hangings, samplers, bookmarks, ring-bearer pillows, and bell pulls. Who knows, if you make a bell pull, a butler may answer!

In our present so-called rat race, needlepoint often serves as a major form of relaxation. Therapeutically, too, it has many uses. For the arthritic, it can be helpful. For the weight-watcher and heavy smoker, it can be all-absorbing. Needlepoint itself, however, is an addiction. It is intriguing, fascinating, and at times, almost too absorbing. The pleasure of watching a design come to life through the addition of one or more bright colors is like that of seeing a rainbow develop before your eyes. Each needleful of yarn makes the design more interesting and the worker more reluctant to put it down.

Equipment

The equipment needed for needlepoint is minimal. The hobby of fishing presumably requires only a piece of string, a bent pin with worm, and a toe. It can, however, soon lure the enthusiast into the purchase of balanced rods, precision reels, and a tackle box that makes Tiffany's window look drab. Needlepoint, on the other hand, requires only some yarn and a piece of canvas; a needle or two, in case one is lost; a thimble, if you use one; and a pair of scissors.

Selecting Canvas

Needlepoint will last only as long as the canvas, so the selection of quality canvas is of first importance. There are two kinds of canvas weaves involved: Penelope, a double weave; and mono-mesh, a single weave.

The Penelope, or double mesh, is a cotton canvas in which double strands run vertically and horizontally forming alternating large and small meshes. It is woven this way to accommodate a small Tent stitch (petit point) in the small holes and a larger Tent stitch (gros point) in the large holes. The worker can therefore use two stitch sizes on one canvas, something that was popular in the early 1900's when scenic designs were in vogue. The fine details of figures and animals were done in petit point and the background in gros point. Penelope is available in eight mesh sizes, the smallest taking 24 stitches to the inch and the largest 3 to the inch, and it is 40 inches wide. All sizes come in ecru and sizes #5 and #3 also come in white; additional double-mesh sizes in white will be marketed soon.

For the average needlepointer, the mono-mesh canvas is preferable. Its threads are evenly spaced in both directions, so the mesh is uniform in size. It is woven from 24 to 3 threads per inch and runs from 36 to 54 inches in width. The number of threads to the inch corresponds to the number of stitches that can be taken in a running inch of canvas. Hence, the fewer threads per inch, the larger the hole and the larger the stitch. Mono-mesh comes in ecru and white. The latter is the most popular today, because the yarn colors contrast well with the background. It is also reportedly easier on the eyes. The design emerges far more dramatically from a white background, and the effect is certainly a lot more exciting than it is from an ecru background.

The major requirements in a good canvas mesh are strong, smooth, polished, evenly spaced threads. Too often we are carried away by the design of a needlepoint piece and forget to examine the material upon which it is painted and upon which we will be working for many weeks. Work done on inferior canvas is hours of wasted effort. A smooth, polished, even thread helps to make a consistently firm, even stitch. The smoothness allows the yarn to glide through the holes without any enforced yanking, whereas a harsh, unpolished thread will catch the yarn in the mesh and split it as it goes through. Sizing is added to all good canvas, not to reinforce the thread but to give it body and smoothness. If there is too much sizing, however, it will be like working on a gunny sack; if there is too little, it will be like playing with a rag doll.

All canvas has knots, and knots make bumps. Unfortunately a canvas thread cannot extend forever. It must be joined to another thread somewhere. Hopefully, that will be in the margin area, but just make certain that the thread doesn't end and the knot come plumb in the middle of the most prominent part of the design.

When selecting a canvas design or a piece of canvas for a design, you should always be sure that there is, or that you have allowed for, a margin of between 1½ to 2½ inches for tacks when blocking and for "tuck-in" when mounting the needlepoint.

Selecting Yarn and Other Materials

Throughout history, most canvas embroidery has been done in wool because of its availability and its durability. Needlepoint needs a long fibered yarn like wool which will not split when pulled through an endless series of holes. There are three satisfactory kinds of yarns, especially manufactured for needlepoint, available in America today: Persian, tapestry, and rug.

The Golden Fleece of them all is Persian. But although imported, it never set a cloven hoof in Persia. It gets its name from its close resemblance to the yarn used in the beautiful Sarouk and Kirman rugs. Its popularity lies in its glossiness, adaptability to the canvas weave, and rainbow range of colors. It has a necessary resilience not found in other wools. A 3-ply yarn, it is easily divided for use in different size canvas meshes. All wool, mothproof, and color-fast, it comes when

uncut in ¼-pound hanks. Usually, however, it is purchased in a needlework shop or department store where it has been cut into convenient 34-inch lengths. It is also sometimes packaged in small uncut skeins and 40-yard skeins. It does not fray or shred, a rather important factor in anything that may get rugged use.

Tapestry yarn, a 4-ply wool that comes in 40-yard skeins, is rugged, makes a smooth stitch, and slides through the mesh well. But it has a more muted luster than Persian yarn, and as it is tightly twisted, it cannot be separated for use in smaller meshes. Rug yarn, much thicker and rougher than the others, comes in ½-pound hanks and is naturally only suitable for very large mesh.

The use of such substitutes as knitting and crocheting yarns is not recommended. These yarns are made of shorter fibers and will not withstand the constant rubbing against the coarse canvas threads.

There are other interesting materials being used in needlepoint today, and fascinating effects can be obtained with them by using a combination of different ones. Silk, for instance, is lovely used either as an entire ground or for an accent in a design with wool. French silk is particularly recommended for needlepoint. There are 9 yards in each skein and 7 strands to the thread. When used in full strength, it covers a 14 threads to the inch canvas mesh beautifully. It is possible to separate it to fit other mesh sizes, although this is a little tedious as the strands are apt to snag. French silk is not twisted like needlepoint wool yarns, so it takes more guidance to pull the thread through and have it lie flat on the surface. A certain rhythmic twist develops when working with it, and the results are worth this added effort. It is durable, though in this respect no other medium can surpass wool, and so far it is expensive to use.

Embroidery cotton can also be used with satisfaction. It has 6 strands to the thread. When used full ply, it is perfect for a 16 threads to the inch canvas. Embroidery cotton, which has been mercerized, has a polish that shines even more than French silk. If colorfast, it will be so labeled. It comes in small skeins of over 8 yards to the skein.

Gold and silver metallic threads are also available, and are fine for surface work, for outlining, and for small accent areas. None has yet been sufficiently perfected to use satisfactorily in large areas as these threads tend to fray or break. Raffia makes a good texture, and that made from synthetics is strong. However, the stitch pattern must cover a fair-sized area as raffia is roughly ¼ inch wide. Other materials such as wire, beads, feathers, shells, and stones are all part of the creative embroidery trend. Shells and stones are appliquéd on the surface, held in place by an enmeshing loop stitch. Some are in good taste and add to a design, but there is the risk of having them look too contrived.

If texture is a requirement, a knowledgeable selection of needlepoint stitch patterns can often accomplish as much as a change in material. But it is hard to beat the texture of a real feather or the reflection of light on a glass bead.

Yarn Requirements

In trying to determine the amount of yarn needed to cover a given piece of canvas, it is always wise to buy more than you think you require, because there may well be a difference in the dye lots by the time you discover you need to purchase a second batch. Sometimes this difference is very slight, but in a large area even the slightest change will be perceptible when the yarn is worked into the canvas. Blues are particularly risky in this respect. It is therefore only sensible to take the precaution of buying too much rather than too little. Yarn need never be wasted. When the yarn bag in the linen closet starts to displace the sheets, it is time to work a patchwork or geometric design with the leftovers.

The length of cut yarn found in needlepoint shops—around 34 inches—is just the proper size for a working strand, and using the Tent stitch on #10 and #12 mesh canvas, it will cover one square inch. Some stitches take more yarn than others, but the increase is very slight. If you are using #12 and #14 mesh canvas and 2-ply yarn, the yarn requirement will be slightly less since the separated ply from one strand is combined with the separated ply from another to make the needed 2-ply strand. The average pillow, 14 by 14 inches in size, worked on #12 or #14 canvas threads to the inch, requires 5 to 6 ounces.

Canvas and Yarn Coverage

Unlike some of our contemporary paintings, needlepoint is not enhanced by exposed canvas. Canvas threads that show are sloppy.

There is no hard and fast rule determining what weight yarn should be used with what size mesh, particularly when you are working with ornamental stitches that vary in the way they cover the canvas. Generally, if the mesh shows, the thread is too thin, if the stitch looks bulky, the thread is too thick. It is always a good idea to begin by working a small sample square on a practice piece or on the edge of the canvas. Tension varies with each worker. The looser one works, the better the stitch will cover. Different colors, too, may vary in weight, with the darker colors usually running thinner. If used more loosely, these thinner yarns may cover better, and it will not be necessary to increase the number of strands.

If too bulky a yarn is used, the holes in the mesh are enlarged, and the canvas becomes distorted. This can become a tragic experience because the distortion may not show up until the last third of the work. If it takes a hefty yank to pull a stitch through a hole, the yarn is too thick.

Upright stitches do not cover the canvas as well as angle or slanting stitches because they leave exposed the canvas intersections between them. If you are using Persian yarn, it is therefore generally necessary to use one more ply of yarn or a smaller holed mesh when working any upright stitch.

Some stitches or stitch patterns expose the canvas more readily than others. This is particularly apparent in some of the Gobelin stitches. The easy remedy of using a heavier yarn does not always work, so to keep a fine stitch and avoid the bulky army-sock look, a color corresponding to the yarn color must be painted on the canvas surface. Try your stitch on the canvas. If it doesn't cover, take out the trial stitches; then with a small paintbrush, touch up the front of the area with paint.

To paint a canvas surface, acrylics or oil paints are recommended. Acrylics are more satisfactory because they can be thinned with water. Oil paint requires turpentine as a thinner, and sometimes the addition of just the slightest amount too much will cause the paint to blot over a large area of canvas. Test the oil paint in the margin before applying it to the design area and wait a minute or two, because blotting does not always occur immediately. Only a very small amount of color is necessary to cover the canvas, and duplicating the exact color value is not necessary. Magic Markers must be used with the utmost caution and are not recommended for filling in large areas. Even those tested with boiling water may not run in a small test piece but may take off like the Johnstown flood when used in large areas.

The chart opposite is a guide for telling what size yarn to use with what size canvas mesh. It does not attempt to cover every circumstance, but it is good as a general rule of thumb. It refers to Persian yarn and mono-mesh canvas only, the most popular and most commonly used materials.

To cover Penelope canvas, the size most commonly used, requires 10 large stitches to the inch or 20 small ones. Use a 3-ply Persian yarn for the large holes and 1-ply yarn for the small. Crewel wool for the latter could also be used.

Needlepoint tapestry yarn comes in the desired width for the large stitch on this same Penelope canvas, so no adjustment in thickness is necessary.

For the Bargello stitches, I recommend using a canvas size #14 threads to the inch or #13 if it is available. Though #12 is recommended by many for Bargello patterns, I find that the canvas threads show, no matter how carefully or loosely the stitches are worked. However, if larger mesh and a larger stitch is desired, the yarn must be increased in thickness. If you are using Persian yarn, cut all strands the same length, try a 3-ply strand, and add however many more strands are required to cover the canvas acceptably. They will work together smoothly as the fibers in Persian yarn seem to make one strand adhere to another.

The chart for Bargello patterns is based on mono-mesh canvas sizes and Persian yarn.

With embroidery thread or French silk, use full ply on #16 canvas.

CANVAS, YARN, AND NEEDLE CHART

Canvas Mesh per inch	Number of Ply to Use	Needle Size
#10	3	18, 19
#12	2	19
	3 for dark background	19
#14	2	20, 21
#16	2 for small area	21
	1 with painted surface	23
#18 to #24	1	23, 24
#5 (Penelope)	2 full-ply strands	13
#3	rug yarn, 2 strands	13

BARGELLO PATTERNS

Canvas Mesh Size per Inch	Number of Ply to Use	Stitches requiring heavier yarn	Stitches requiring a painted canvas surface if general table is followed
#10	5	Bargello or Florentine	Brick
#12	4	Hungarian	Upright Gobelin
#13	3	Phulkari	Plaited Gobelin
#14	3	Shadow Box	Large Cross with
#16	2	Diagonal Cretan	Straight Cross
#18	2	St. George & St. Andrew	Double Cross
Any size smaller	1		Chain

Selecting Colors

Selecting colors from a yarn bin for a needlepoint project is like facing a cart of French pastries—they look so good it is hard not to take them all. Perhaps it was easier at the turn of the century when "Victorian black" was the standard back-ground color or in the twenties when the prestitched floral centers were usually surrounded by a "background beige."

We must have a keyboard upon which to tune our choice of colors. There are four points to keep in mind. The first, of course, is availability. The second is personal preference, which in a sense is wholly a matter of personal taste. The third is how the colors will blend with the other furnishings in a room or an outfit of clothing, and the fourth is how they will look together. This last factor is the most important. You can consult a color wheel or a decorator, but if that isn't convenient, there is a phrase that has helped me out of many a frustrating experience—"Something light, something bright, something dark and something neutral." The "neutral" is the stabilizer. Even in the most garish of fabrics, the neutral color is always there. The dullish companion makes the neighboring colors take on value, whether brighter, lighter, darker, or duller.

The number of colors available in needlepoint yarn is staggering. Persian yarn has a color range rivaling a Breughel painting—over 300 colors with up to six shades to a color. French silk comes in over 500 colors with as many as twenty-four shades to a color. Embroidery cotton has a selection of 324 colors with as many as ten to twelve shades to a color. Tapestry and rug yarns have a lesser choice, about 54 colors with four to five shades to each color, but surely a sufficient range to satisfy the requirements of every good design or pattern.

In spite of such a wide choice there will be instances, however, when no color on the chart is satisfactory. It may be a color used by a certain artist, such as Matisse's favorite pink, or a shade as-sociated with certain motifs such as a Chinese blue. We must then make these shades the way a painter does when he mixes paints by combining one strand of one color with one strand of another. Sometimes a heather-like color such as found in Scotch yarns will result, but if the combined colors are similar in value, though different in hue, they will blend together nicely, making a good solid third color.

In a professionally designed piece of needlepoint, the colors are usually indicated on the canvas. These colors may be followed absolutely, or they may be followed up to a point and then one dominant area changed to a shade or even a color more in keeping with whatever decor the article is to be used with. Or the dominant color may be changed entirely, or all the colors may be changed, or simply their tonal value may be changed. This can all be done satisfactorily as long as the yarn chosen covers the design color completely. You are therefore always wise to try out the new yarn color over the painted surface, using one of the stitches you've selected, to make sure that the canvas will be covered before making a definite decision.

In some designs there are spaces and background areas that have been purposely left unpainted, so that the worker can use whatever color fits in with a prescribed decor or outfit. In this case, simply introduce any color that you consider a necessary ingredient to round out the required color scheme.

The Design Element in Needlepoint Stitches

A needlepoint design should be a personal friend. In making your selection, just be sure that you pick one you think will give you pleasure to develop, one you can hardly wait to start, or the piece will never be completed and will be stuffed into the linen closet, forgotten until tag-sale day. Like a friend, your design will be with you for a long time, so choose one you like.

A fine design says a lot in itself, and the choice of stitches to be worked on it should help it to say more, not simply pile on more decoration. It is wise to think of the Tent stitch as the basic ingredient and the other stitches as the embellishment. To put it another way, the Tent stitch is the plum pudding, and the ornamental stitches are the hard sauce. So when selecting stitches for a design, practice caution and restraint. As most designs sold in shops are adaptable to the use of ornamental stitches, no concerted effort need be put into ferreting out a particular type of design. Although the needle cannot hope to match the subtleties, latitudes, and free form achieved by the paintbrush, there are many variables in ornamental stitches that constitute design elements. There are hundreds of stitches making many

different shapes and textures, and creating varying degrees of light intensity, as well as hundreds of colors of yarn that may be used with these stitches to add distinction to a needlepoint design.

Knowing how to do the stitch is certainly the primary requirement, but even more important to good design comes the next step—where to use the stitch once it is learned, something that cannot be adequately mastered by looking at a diagram or an instruction sheet. Although the general appearance of a stitch may influence your decision, the key factors in selecting a stitch are knowing what it can do, what its qualities are, how it will fill an area, and what distinguishes it from other stitches. There are only two ways of finding out: working the stitch out on a practice piece of canvas or seeing it as a design element in a finished piece. Referring to the stitches in the photographs of the finished projects that follow, you can see that there are many characteristics that distinguish one stitch from another: size, shape, direction, practicality, durability, and intricacy. There are also less obvious characteristics that give them individuality. Different stitches reflect different light values and have different textures. They can be grouped to fill in areas of a shape or a background, or they can make a shape themselves as a stitch unit. For instance, the triangular shape of the Rococo stitch can be worked side by side, each stitch fitting into the other to form a solid area, or it can be used alone to represent a leaf or any other triangular shape in a design. Stitches either cover a large area well or are at their best in the confines of a small section of design. They may appear rough next to a smooth stitch and smooth next to a rough stitch.

There are three important qualities to consider in choosing a stitch, which may not appear too obvious—depth, texture, and tactile quality. As I have already mentioned, the placing of one stitch upon another forms a stitch unit and the way in which these stitches are compiled, or the order in which one lies on top of another, will affect their general appearance. Those stitches at the top will reflect more light and be more noticeable than those buried at the bottom. By this interplay of light, many variations in the color of a single shade of yarn can occur. This gradation of color is, of course, very subtle. For a more striking degree of color change, the stitches on the bottom should be worked in a darker shade. Bumpy and overlapping stitches, such as the various cross-stitches, show up this feature of color change to a particularly marked degree. The Diagonal Straight Cross is a good example of several layers of stitches worked atop each other, forming a stitch unit with depth. The Herringbone stitch illustrates the depth in overlapping stitches. The Cretan stitch builds up a center spine.

The second quality to look for in a stitch is texture. Different textures can also be achieved by placing one stitch on top of another, and the variation in weaves that can be created by this means would rival any tweed shop in Scotland.

Closely related to texture is the tactile quality or sensitivity to the touch, that favorite of art critic Bernard Berenson. Some stitches feel as soft as velvet; others as scratchy as old Pullman-car seats. You should be influenced in your choice of stitches as much by the way a stitch feels as by the way it looks. Learning to recognize these three qualities is helpful in selecting the stitch you would like to use in a given area of your needlepoint design.

Once the selection of one stitch for a specific area has been made, it then becomes the exciting decision to choose congenial friends to take adjoining positions. Using contrasting neighboring stitches is always a good rule to follow. As a high building looks higher next to a short one, so a stitch with a high pile will look more elevated next to a smooth, flat stitch. Similarly a smooth, flat stitch next to a textured one will make the latter look rougher, and vice versa. An example of this would be the high pile of the Turkey Knot next to the smooth flatness of the Tent stitch, illustrated in the Tiger-Cat Pillow project (page 100), or the roughness of the Mosaic stitch next to the Encroached Gobelin in the Telephone-Book Cover project (page 88). But often this sculptured look may not be wanted, and then it is possible to use a choice of smooth but dissimilar stitches throughout.

Below is a table to serve as a general guide in making stitch selections. Some stitches are interchangeable and cannot be categorized.

BACKGROUND STITCHES

Upright Stitches

Parisian
Hungarian
Florentine
Bargello
Upright Encroached
    Gobelin
Split Encroached
    Gobelin
Brick

Slanting Stitches

Tent Stitches—
    Continental and
    Basket Weave
Encroached Gobelin
Scotch
Mosaic
Cashmere
Milanese
Oriental
Moorish
Herringbone
Byzantine
Staggered Cross
Ray
Stacked Cube
Basket Weave
    Reverse side

DESIGN AREA FILLERS

Straight Cross
St. George & St. Andrew
Double Straight Cross
Smyrna
Rice
Fern
Couching
Rococo

Satin
Byzantine
Knitting
Leaf
Tip of Leaf
Algerian Eye
Star
Turkey Knot

STITCH UNITS THAT MAKE SHAPES

Fern—ovals and stripes
Round Couching—
    circles
Scotch—squares
Cashmere—rectangles
Byzantine—zigzags
Jacquard—zigzags
Moorish—zigzags
Cretan—ovals
Leaf—ovals
Fishbone—stripes
Tip of Leaf—triangles

Algerian Eye—circles
Star—small circles
Shadow Box—squares
Stacked Cube—
    3-D boxes
Sheaf—bunches
Rococo—bunches or
    triangles
Ray—squares
French Knot—small
    circles
Spider Web—circles

BORDER STITCHES

Long-Armed Cross
Mosaic
Jacquard
Moorish
Algerian Eye (Square)
Shadow Box
Sheaf
Ray
Cashmere
Leviathan

OUTLINE STITCHES

Tent
Back Stitch
Chain
Buttonhole

ACCENT STITCHES—RAISED

Double Straight Cross
Smyrna Cross
Crossed Mosaic
Leviathan
French Knot
Spider Web
Upright Cross

STITCHES FOR SHADING

Tent
Straight Encroached Gobelin
Slanting Encroached Gobelin
Satin

RUG STITCHES

Long-Armed Cross
Herringbone
Knitting
Staggered Cross

LOOP STITCHES

Chain
Buttonhole
Turkey Knot

Now let us see what we can do with a simple design and some of these ornamental stitches. We have chosen a rather prosaic still life, something that can often be found in a wall hanging. It is a bouquet of flowers in a vase. Some of the flowers are round like cabbage roses; others have large petals; and some are wispy like daisies. The vase is cone-shaped and worked in a single color. The background is plain. This design has little character or individuality, but we can play Pygmalion and give it personality by using some of the ornamental stitches in our repertoire. We can make the display impressionistic, realistic, fanciful, or contemporary. We can make the flowers fuzzy or smooth, rounded or angular. We can treat it like Van Gogh's "Sunflowers" using lots of texture in the stitches to simulate his brush strokes, or make it into an eighteenth-century bouquet with fuzzy stitch detail and lots of exaggerated swirls or into nineteenth-century English watercolor with delicate tapestry-like stitches. We can be even more daring and make a cubist interpretation in the Picasso manner. In that case, we may have to go beyond the outlines of the drawing, making angles where there are curves, but this, too, can easily be done.

Our choice of colors will follow those indicated in the design, but we'll change the tone values. In the Postimpressionist picture, the colors should be as brilliant and as sunlike as our yarn palette will allow. In the French bouquet, they should be as bright and clear as real spring flowers. The English watercolor should be muted in color, and the cubist interpretation an interplay of dark and light forming unusual forms.

Let's start with the technique of Van Gogh. There is no restraint or regimentation in his work. He heaped on paint with large brushstrokes the way we would like to frost a cake. This use of strong bold strokes should be a delight to try to emulate with our ornamental stitches. We'll begin with the flowers. The round cabbage roses should have a stitch that will fill their area by going in an unregimented fashion in many directions. In looking at the projects that follow, we can see that the stitches used for the scales of the fish on the Jiffy Tote Bag (page 81) can be maneuvered in such a way that they work well in a group. There are Leaf and Tip of Leaf stitches, and they can be worked horizontally, vertically, and diagonally, so that they can follow the outlines of the flowers' round form with only minor irregularities. As for color, Van Gogh used several shades of one color in a single flower and often threw in an opposing color. If the flower is to be yellow, three or four shades of yellow could be used with an occasional leaf unit of soft blue. For the large petaled flower, we need a stitch that will make an oval. In looking through the illustrations and diagrams again, we find that the Cretan stitch in the Chinese-Butterfly Pillow (page 104) can go in three directions, making nice oval forms. It also has a raised look along the spine that resembles brushstrokes. It can be widened or narrowed to fit the size of the petals. Only one color should be used for these petals as each petal is made up of just one stitch unit. For the daisy-like flower, we want a thin, spiny leaf form that can be used in many directions, so that we can make the petals radiate from a center axis. The Fern stitch used on the Jacobean Pillow (page 118)

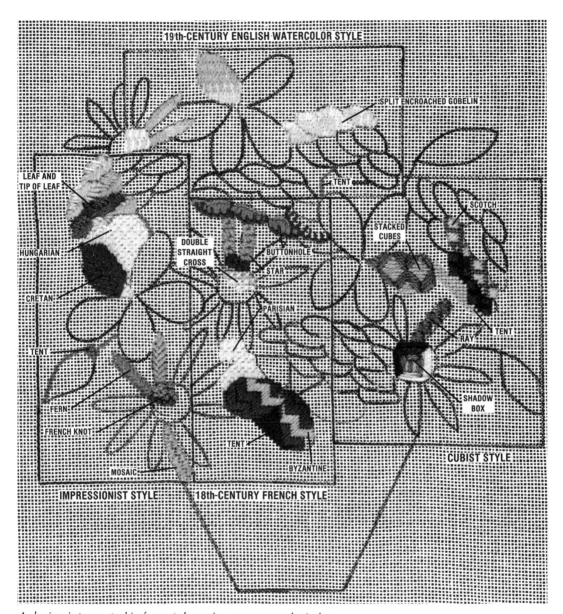

A design interpreted in four styles using ornamental stitches

forms a compact stitch that fills the bill nicely; it is firm, slim, and can be worked in three directions. Van Gogh would probably give the daisy a pretty prickly center, so one of the stitches in our "Accent" group would be appropriate. Any of the Cross stitches or the French Knots could form a cluster. The leaves and stems should be worked in the Tent stitch, as we now have enough activity going on in the flowers for even a Van Gogh painting. The vase should be flat in appearance, so only one color should be used with no shading required, but it should have some texture. Good choices would be the Cashmere stitch used for the Bicycle-Seat Cover (page 49), or the Mosaic stitch used for the Telephone-Book Cover (page 88). The units of these stitches when worked in a series form an interesting boxlike pattern. The background must have some texture, too, but in a fairly quiet way since we already have a swirl of activity and color working. An upright background stitch in a neutral putty shade might be a nice relief. The Hungarian is a good choice because it forms a pattern of short, upright brushstrokes. It has texture, but it is a delicate texture as one can see in the Byzantine Eyeglass Case (page 94). Our still life may not duplicate Van Gogh's, but it has some of the same mood and spirit.

If we take the original still life and give it a French twist, we would want perhaps again to accentuate the flowers, making them extravagantly colorful the way a painter can make a bouquet look as if it smelled good. The style should be naturalistic but done with great precision in an ornate way. The cabbage rose this time could be delicately shaded in at least two shades of one color and worked in one of the loop stitches that swing around curves so nicely. The edging on two of the flowers in the Jacobean Pillow (page 118) are done in the Buttonhole stitch and worked in two closely related shades. Each petal in this layered rose could be treated as a single object with the length of the Buttonhole stitches adjusting to the curve of the petal. The large petaled flower requires a smooth stitch so that each petal can be worked in various lengths and shades. The smooth Byzantine stitch would work well for a poppy or anemone-type flower and allow the use of a different shade in each row. In the Byzantine Eyeglass Case (page 94) it is used as a background stitch, but it need not be worked as such. The daisy should be dainty and would look sweet done in a series of Star stitches radiating from a center section done in the Double Straight Cross. These stitches are worked in small units and can be placed in staggered fashion to form a slender daisy petal. Again in the Byzantine Eyeglass Case, these minute dainty stitches can be seen. The vase should be beautifully shaded in as many shades of one color as are available with a very definite highlight placed in one small section. The Tent stitch is suggested for this and for the leaves and stems as well. For the background, which should recede into quiet elegance from all the flamboyance of color and design in the other areas, the dignified upright stitches of the Parisian, used in one of the squares of the Chinese-Patchwork Footstool (page 110), would be perfect, particularly in some of the lovely pale shades of French blue, green or rose.

For the English watercolor treatment

we would work the still life in carefully muted shades of the colors designated in the design. A picture quiet in mood should be quiet in color and texture, with nothing dominant in the composition. These muted colors require the smoothness of some of the more subtle stitches. The Split Encroached Gobelin stitch used for the orchid shapes in the Telephone-Book Cover (page 88) is smooth and tranquil and easily adapted to intricate shading. Using it for all the flowers and the vase will give the composition that Old World quality found in English prints. The leaves, stems, and background could then be worked in the Tent stitch. Or we might reverse these stitches and have the flowers and vase shaded in the Tent stitch and the leaves and background in the Split Encroached Gobelin.

To do the still life in a cubist style is to work with crazy-quilt shapes. Although none of the stitch units need conform to the petal shape of the flowers, they should follow the contour of the floral outline as much as possible. No attempt at realism is expected, and the colors selected need not always follow those used in the original design. Guitar or violin browns, black, white, and gray will be appropriate. The cabbage-rose flower could be done in the Scotch stitch in a series of small squares as shown in the graph of the Scotch-Stitch Pillow (page 35). Each square could be done either in a different or in related shades of brown. With the Scotch stitch we could never hope to make a circle no matter how cleverly the units are grouped, but disregarding the petal lines of the interior, the general form of the flower could be followed. The jagged edges of the angles of

the square will in itself add the contour look we are trying for. The large petaled flower could be worked in the Stacked Cube stitch in black, white, and gray, decreasing the sides of the boxes as the shapes taper at each end. The Stacked Cube stitch used for the Bookends (page 85) gives an idea of how this can be done. If it seems too contrived for your taste, try filling the area of the large petals with the Flame stitch (described on page 67) worked in the same colors of black, white, and gray. The Ray stitch radiating from a center could make the petals of the daisy. The border of the Chinese-Butterfly Pillow (page 104) shows us the Ray stitch going in two directions with the rays bursting from a corner. They can fan out in all directions. The center of the daisy could be done in one single Shadow Box stitch unit, and both center and petals could be in shades of gray from light to dark. The vase would be smashing done in the Jacquard or the Moorish stitch, shown in the Chinese-Patchwork Footstool (page 110), in a reddish brown with a black bordering stitch to the unit. Something light in color but flat as a pancake is needed for the background. The Tent stitch in a warm buff color would be effective. By keeping our palette deliberately low key, we insure that there will be no distraction from the unusual shapes.

We have experimented with one very ordinary design, giving it four different faces, but any design can accommodate and be enhanced by decorative stitches. We may not always purchase a representational design. There are many beautiful geometric patterns available that are very popular with needlepointers, particularly because the shapes and colors change so rapidly there is a lot of action and variety to the work. The interest span of many needleworkers approximates that of a new puppy, and this is understandable where there are such fascinating temptations just a few inches away.

If you look at an old quilt, you will see that there are often small touches in the design that veer from the normal pattern, adding charm and whimsy to the patterns so diligently and faithfully followed by our grandparents. On the wall in front of me as I write is a crazy quilt made of many different pieces of silks and satins in an assortment of jewel-like colors. All of the "crazy" shapes fit into each other with the ease of a kaleidoscope. One little irregular square is casually placed off center; it is a full-blown rose beautifully embroidered in silk thread, the only piece of surface embroidery on the entire quilt other than the Feather stitch edging each piece. One could say it is out of keeping with the rest of the quilt, but to me it is a romantic addition to an already lovely object. This is what a few ornamental stitches can do for a geometric design.

As an example, let's take an American Indian motif, a center design surrounded by lots of triangles and other angles, with the background area becoming part of the design. There are many ways to adapt this design, but for our purposes we'll treat it in just three ways: smooth as in a deerhide, textured and furry as in a buffalo robe, and decorative as in a ceremonial costume of beads and feathers. The deerhide look requires a smooth treatment throughout, and the Encroached Gobelin stitch could be used for design as well as background. There are, however, some lovely border stitches that could outline the geometric forms with a neat handsome braid and would still be in keeping with the Indian motif. Most geometric shapes in an Indian design have an outline of one or two different colors. On the Bordered Handbag (page 58), the Long-Armed Cross stitch is used in this way. It is trim and handsome, and can be worked around the pointed angles of this design.

For the buffalo-robe look, the Turkey Knot stitch simulates fur beautifully as illustrated in the Tiger-Cat Pillow project (page 100). If this stitch covered the entire surface of the canvas, it would make a quite sensational rug. In early American homes, the "Turkey Work" runner on a table was as much a part of the household establishment as the indigo pot in the back shed. On a small piece, however, rather than have the whole design in Turkey Knot, it would look more attractive to use it for only small portions, and to do the rest in the Tent stitch.

We are all acquainted with the intricate beadwork used by the Indians on their ceremonial robes and leather trinkets. For our third interpretation of the Indian motif, we could use actual beads on our needlework if we so chose. Beads look best in small areas on small needlepoint pieces. In the Victorian era, needlepoint featured lots of beadwork as a design element on a cross-stitch background. The technique is to slip the beads on the needle with each Tent stitch, using a slender needle. For the feathered look also, we could incorporate the actual feathers into the yarn. The only trick is keeping the quill well secured on the back of the work, while the feathers are fastened on top with the Tent stitch. These are, however, rather

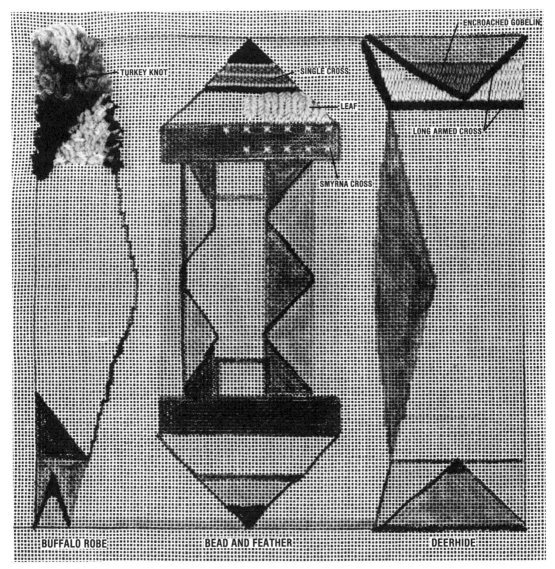

Ornamental stitches creating different textures

contrived, gimmicky methods, and there are ornamental stitches that can create something similar in appearance to these trimmings. The Single Cross stitch worked over one thread gives a lovely beadlike look and can be used in large areas as well as small. The Smyrna Cross stitch makes a slightly more raised and heavier cross, and it also can be used in large or small areas of design. Both of these stitches are represented in the Address Book cover (page 39). The French Knot is good, too, but is more successfully worked in small areas, as it is difficult to make the knots consistent over a sizable clump. As Indian beadwork was often used as a trim, rather than for extensive areas of design, using an accent cluster of bead stitches here and there would be effective. The feather can be represented by the Leaf stitch, which as a stitch unit looks like one. The Cretan would do well, too, as it even has a center spine. Color in the American Indian palette was mostly primary, although the earliest pieces of deerhide work are painted in red, ocher, black, and white.

All these examples of design interpretation are only to be used as guidelines in selecting stitches for whatever needlepoint design you plan to work. The hope is that they will release you from the bonds of one or two repetitive stitches, point you to new methods of approach, and open up a new world of creative needlepoint.

PART TWO

TWENTY NEEDLEPOINT PROJECTS

There are people who fairly boast that they cannot follow a diagram, that their minds snap shut when they see graphs and numbers. It is, however, my firm belief that if you can master the panel of an ordinary cooking stove, you can follow a diagram for the most difficult of canvas-embroidery stitches. The diagrams that follow are clearly numbered in sequence of stitch use. The base of the arrow shaft indicates where the needle comes out of the canvas, and the number and the arrowhead indicate where the needle goes in.

Sometimes stitches do not dovetail or mesh properly, usually around a design or at the edges of a border, so that the canvas intersections are exposed. Then compensating stitches are needed. They should be smaller stitches, maneuverable in small spaces, and follow the direction of the larger stitches. Compensating or filler stitches are indicated by a broken line.

Instructions and diagrams for left-handed needleworkers are given only when the general instructions might present a problem for them.

Note: In the following projects, I used white mono-mesh canvas and Persian yarn throughout, unless otherwise indicated. A photograph of the finished article either in color or black and white, a photograph of the unworked canvas design, and a closeup of the worked ornamental stitches are included in every case.

Pillow in Marble Pattern

Tent Stitch—Continental, Basket Weave

This pillow resembling a piece of marble is an example of how the basic needlepoint stitch, the **Tent** stitch, can be worked in two different ways in the same design. One method is the **Continental**; the other, the **Basket Weave**. The design is worked on #14 canvas threads to the inch with 2-ply Persian yarn. Wherever there is an area of three or more diagonal stitches in one color area, the Basket Weave is used. This is recommended to avoid canvas distortion. The Continental, which adapts itself better to small areas and to outlining, is used in the other areas.

Each group of colors I chose for this piece were related but were not intended to be used for shading. Each gradation in color is meant to simulate the striations in marble. Pink, red, and rust were used for one section, and three shades of gray-blue and an oyster white for the other. These colors blend very nicely with Oriental rugs.

A design like this is never monotonous to work. The interplay of stitches and colors keeps the worker busy and interested.

The Tent stitch is the grandmamma of all good canvas embroidery, and despite the lure and developing interest in other fancier stitches, it is the cream of exquisite needlepoint, the basic stitch upon which all other angle stitches are founded. There are three methods of doing the Tent stitch: the Half-Cross (not used in this project), the Continental, and the Basket Weave. Since all three make the same stitch, a needlepoint worker is often puzzled as to just which method is used, but the covering on the back of the canvas will indicate this, as well as its wearing quality. The Half-Cross makes a small vertical stitch barely covering the back of the canvas and should be used only when durability is not a factor; the Continental has a long slanting stitch covering the horizontal weave of the back of the canvas; and the Basket Weave produces a sturdy crisscross weave covering both horizontal and vertical weaves.

Historical references use the term the Tent stitch, whereas a modern worker often refers to it by the name of the method or calls it just plain "needlepoint." The origin of the name is cloaked in mystery. Some say that this stitch was actually used on tents, but whether for decoration or for whipping the flaps together in Omar Khayyám fashion is never divulged. We do know that specimens of it were found on remnants of cloth in some Egyptian tombs of the fifteenth century B.C. and that it was used in Rome on garments before the time of the Caesars; but these were all surface embroidery stitches. It was the Chinese, those ancient lovers of beauty, who first used the Tent stitch as a form of canvas embroidery, and it is thought to have originated there in the twelfth century and been introduced to the Western world about a hundred years later. After achieving great popularity in Germany in the sixteenth century, it was imported to England, the embroidery center of the modern world. There it was first called the "Cushion" stitch and used on church appointments and even, perhaps, cushions. Today it is still famous as "cushion" stitch to the thousands of needlepointers who use it to cover pillows.

The Moravians brought the Tent stitch to America from Germany in the early eighteenth century, and examples of it can be seen in our museums today. It was used mainly as a surface embroidery stitch on silk or satin pictures of bereaved families mourning over the graves of their loved ones. In the restored buildings of the cloister in Ephrata, Pennsylvania, that hub of embroidery, one can see the dimly lit cells, row after row, where the sisters of Ephrata stitched their famous work. On the windowsill of one of the buildings, which was in the process of being restored, I saw a darling little canvas-embroidery pincushion with a six-pointed star done in the Tent and the Smyrna Cross.

Both in the past and today we find the most beautiful work done in the Tent stitch. It was the first stitch to attract attention to needlepoint as an art medium and still remains the most popular of all canvas-embroidery stitches. All methods of the Tent stitch cover a single cross-weave of canvas on the diagonal, usually slanting from left to right.

The Continental is an important form of the Tent stitch that all needleworkers should learn. It is essential for small areas, for fine work, and for making compensating stitches, that is, filling in around other kinds of slanting stitches or stitch patterns where the canvas is not covered. The Continental is the most popular of the three Tent stitch methods, although perhaps the most monotonous of needlepoint stitches when used on large areas. It is really not the ideal background stitch and is much too frequently used as such. Worked in horizontal rows, the canvas must be completely turned around at each boundary in order to have the stitches follow the same angle as the previous row. The long stitch that it makes on the back of the canvas, going

Tent stitches: Continental and Basket Weave

only in one direction, tends to form horizontal ridges on the front, in addition to pulling the canvas out of shape. The ridges and distortion fortunately are not apparent in small areas, and when used for and around such areas in a design, the stitch is indispensable.

The Basket Weave is preferred by many needlepoint enthusiasts for background use and for solid areas of design. It is worked diagonally whereas other versions of the Tent stitch are worked horizontally or vertically. This means there is a change in weave direction in each row, so it puts no strain on the canvas and hence causes no distortion or ridges in the work. The result is a series of soft, smooth diagonal stitches on the front and a beautiful basket weave design on the back. The canvas does not have to be switched around, and the design turned upside down, at the end of every other row, which makes working conditions more agreeable.

CONTINENTAL

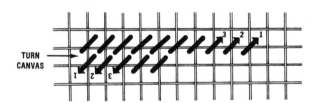

TURN CANVAS

This stitch is worked from right to left across the canvas. Starting from the right, bring the needle out at the lower left of a boundary intersection, passing over the intersection at upper right. Bring the needle out 2 threads to the left and 1 thread down. The next stitch is a repeat; angle over the intersection, pass under 2 vertical threads, and out. This will make a long diagonal stitch on the back. Work to the end of boundary, then turn your work around for the next row and return to the right boundary.

Left-handed workers should start in upper left-hand corner and work to the right, bringing the needle out at the top right of a boundary intersection, passing over the intersection at the lower right. Then bring the needle out 2 threads to the right and 1 thread up.

BASKET WEAVE

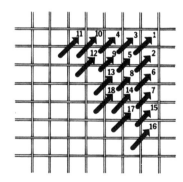

Establish the top and bottom of your work and keep it always in the same position, never turning at the end of a row. To start a corner, make the first stitch at the upper right of the area to be covered. Bring the needle out at the lower left of the intersection to be covered, passing over the intersection at the upper right. Bring needle out directly below the hole where the first stitch was started and pass needle over the intersection at upper right, bringing needle out under 2 vertical threads to the left. For the third stitch, cover the intersection at upper right and come out the hole directly to the side, opposite the bottom of the last stitch, passing the needle over the intersection of the upper right, and bring needle out under 2 horizontal threads below. Pass the thread over the intersection to the upper right and again pass needle under 2 horizontal threads, and bring needle out below. Pass needle over intersection to the upper right and bring needle out *directly* below bottom of last stitch. This will be ending one row and starting another. Pass needle over intersection to upper right and bring needle out 2 threads over to the left, and continue up the stairs. You will be increasing one stitch at the end of each row until the maximum number of stitches for the width is attained.

The needle is straight up and down when descending; it is straight across when ascend-

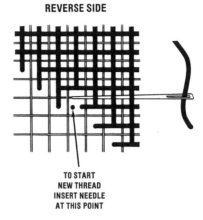

REVERSE SIDE

TO START
NEW THREAD
INSERT NEEDLE
AT THIS POINT

ing; and it is on an angle only when increasing at the end of each row. Each stitch covers the intersection of threads or cross-weave of the canvas. The second diagram shows the reverse side of the canvas. It shows how to end the thread by skimming under the surface of a few stitches. It also shows where to insert the needle to start a new thread from the back of the canvas.

Left-handed workers should start at the bottom left and work to the right, and up.

Chair Seat in Diaper Pattern

Tent Stitch, Diaper Pattern

"Doing the dining-room chairs" is a phrase often uttered by needlepointers. This is a most worthy project, which can give a feeling of personal warmth and beauty to a dining room. Martha Washington, as we have already mentioned, set an example for many an industrious housewife by completing a set of eight chair seats executed in a cross-stitch pattern of scallop shells. A matching set is, of course, the perfect decorating appointment, but it takes enormous discipline. The first two chair seats go rather rapidly, but interest lags and the remaining two, four, or six seem to drag on endlessly.

There are several ways to speed up this endeavor. One very attractive and successful method is to use the same motif in each chair seat but to vary the design. For the seashore enthusiast, a series of different kinds of shells or examples of marine life; for the nature lover, some woodsy motifs; and for the modern city dweller, a geometric or abstract design. Another method is to choose a de-

sign that has very little background; though the same amount of space is covered, somehow working a design is more interesting and goes faster than working background. Or as a background accelerator you can use some of the more rapidly worked background stitches, such as the Mosaic, the Cashmere, and the Parisian. In that case, however, you should understand that though such stitches go more rapidly and are very satisfactory, they do make a heavier pile. So for a delicate design, the Tent stitch is recommended. Also highly recommended for chair seats are Bargello designs, which have been fashionable for many hundreds of years. The stitch moves along swiftly, can be worked in a great variety of many unusual and fascinating patterns and colors, and wears well.

Another beautiful chair seat design is the Diaper Pattern illustrated here. It was a particularly appropriate choice for this Gondola chair, because so many seats of the period were made of cane, and this pattern is reminiscent of

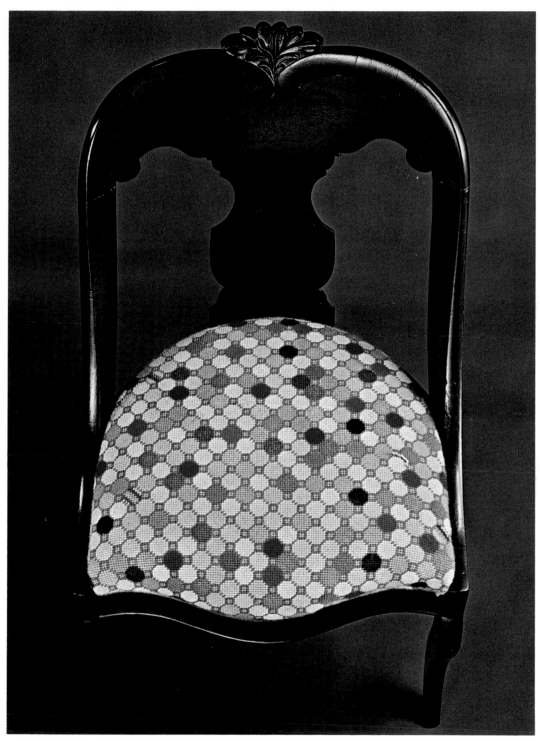

CHAIR SEAT IN DIAPER PATTERN

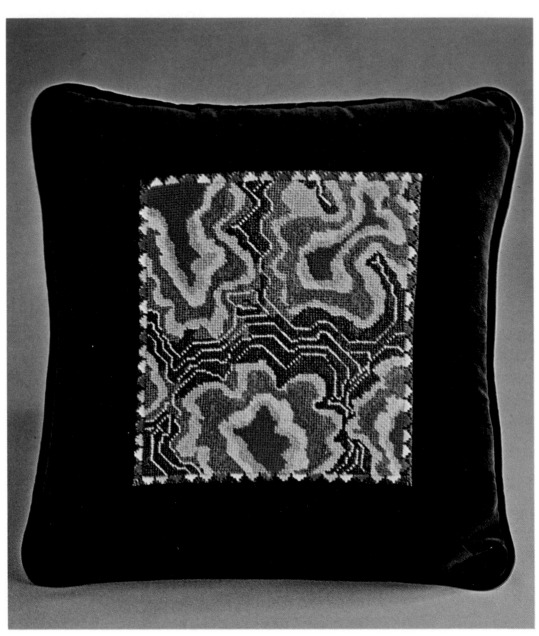

PILLOW IN MARBLE PATTERN

Diaper Pattern

woven cane. It is worked on #10 canvas threads to the inch with 3-ply Persian yarn. No sketch on the canvas or on graph paper is required as the pattern can be easily transcribed by following the outline of the geometric figures which simply repeat themselves and interlock in mosaic fashion. This pattern is one of hundreds using the Tent stitch with one color forming the lattice or outline and other colors forming the interior of each unit. This particular canvas was started in an effort to use up excess yarns with no specific color plan in mind. By working different colors in each unit, the design began to look like a maharani's jewel box.

The word *diaper* was originally a term for a white cloth with a geometric weave, which became more widely associated with the nursery. However, in embroidery circles, it has come to mean a pattern made up of small repeated geometric units covering an entire background. These patterns are also referred to as groundings. Diaper patterns were popular during the Victorian era and many tiny footstools worked in them still exist. Beads were often used as a filler, adding a feminine, gaudy look. The designs themselves are easily devised, and with a little creative effort, the needleworker can become the originator of another new pattern.

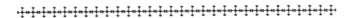

DIAPER PATTERN

Starting from the approximate center of the canvas, work 4 Tent stitches horizontally to the right. Work down 2 stitches diagonally to the right from this line. Work down 3 stitches vertically from this last diagonal stitch. Work 2 stitches diagonally to the left. Work across 3 stitches horizontally to the left from this last diagonal stitch. This forms five sides of the octagonal lattice. From the horizontal and vertical sides of the octagon, work a square with 4 stitches for each side. Continue this lattice throughout the background area.

Scotch-Stitch Pillow

Scotch, Tent Stitches

Not all needlepoint designs have to rival a Matisse painting in color and composition. Just a simple line drawing can sometimes say as much as a fully painted canvas. I have seen a series of blocks done in one color using various ornamental stitches, and it was as striking and appealing as any elaborate, professionally designed piece of work. A plain design with little detail can be very monot-

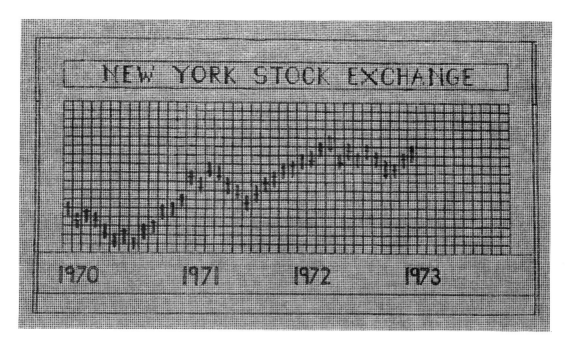

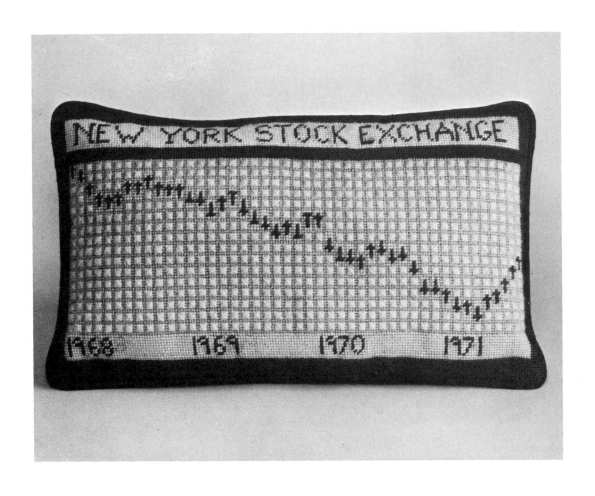

36   **SCOTCH-STITCH PILLOW**

onous to work, but with the use of ornamental stitches, the simplest, most mundane idea can be turned into an exciting challenge.

This graph made into a pillow will get a chuckle, as well as admiration for its general appearance. It is worked on #14 canvas threads to the inch with 2-ply Persian yarn. There are many checkered-type stitches that could be used for the graph squares, but I chose the **Scotch** stitch, because its bumpy effect and box shape give the desired emphasis. It is a series of stitch units of boxes made up of angle stitches, increased and decreased to form a square, framed by the **Tent** stitch. Some box or checkered-type stitches distort the canvas, but in this instance, the pull of the Tent stitch surrounding the square helps to keep the canvas from stretching over to one side. Everything else—border, lettering, and point markers—are worked in the Tent.

The Scotch stitch is most often used as a background or in large sections of a design because of its uniformity and rigid outline. It is most satisfactory when used in a block area, such as the design on this pillow, as the compensating stitches needed along the side of an irregular design would be rather numerous.

The choice of color in this sample design was no problem; it was almost spelled out. I used one shade of a grayish off-white for the graph squares and a darker shade of gray for the graph lines that frame them. The point markers on

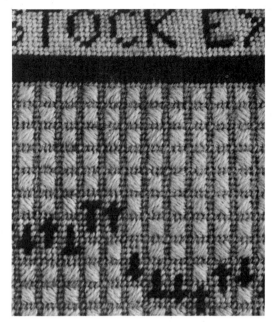

Scotch

the graph (which are worked first) were emphasized and made more dramatic by using a medium-dark blue; any other medium shade would be suitable, however. The lettering was also done in blue. A dull red was used for the border. One might suspect that the red would detract from the ornamental stitching, but instead, it framed the oyster whites of the graph and complemented the blue of the markers. What could have been tedious if done in one basic stitch, turned into a fairly rapid checker game, as well as an interesting study of the stock market's fluctuations.

SCOTCH

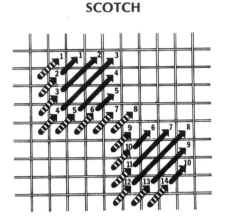

Starting from top, left to right, work a 3-thread square over 1,2,3,2,1, intersections with a slanting stitch, skipping an intersection between each square to accommodate the bordering Tent stitch. Continue these squares going in the same or alternating directions over the entire area to be covered. The squares may be worked in stitch units going from left to right in a horizontal row, or worked in a vertical row, or worked on a diagonal, with the surrounding Tent border worked in later. Once a work pattern is established, however, it is best to stick to it so that the canvas will not warp in some places and remain true in others. There is no hard-and-fast rule for this. It is merely a suggestion, so that blocking will be easier. When working the Tent stitch border, there will be a certain amount of thread dragging on the back of your canvas. It can be worked through the back of the stitches to the next starting point.

Left-handed workers should start at the bottom left of the work, working to the right and up.

Cross-Stitch Address Book

Upright Cross, Rice, Upright Crossed Corners, Smyrna Cross, Double Straight Cross, Staggered Cross, Large with Upright Cross Stitches

There are as many cross-stitches as there are blackbirds in a pie. The patterns they make are quite dissimilar, and one single variation in the direction of the cross can make a startling change in design and texture. Some are like fine lace; others are as rough as burlap. Some make squares; others, diamonds. The only way to ferret out a favorite is to make a sampler of them. Mine was done on #12 canvas threads to the inch in the form of stacked boxes, working in three shades of one color with the lightest on top where the light would strike.

For the average young girl who is exposed to needlework, the first stitch she learns is the cross-stitch. Usually it is taught to her by her grandmother, who learned it from her mother, and that is thought of as its origin. But it can be carried back to the time of the great pharaohs of Egypt in 1200 B.C. In this century, fragments of cloth stitched with a cross-stitch border have been excavated from the burial grounds of the Valley of the Kings in Luxor.

I thought the design of the stacked

Cross-stitches

See color picture opposite page 48

boxes was contemporary, but I later discovered it in a book of ancient illuminated manuscripts. Old or new, it was a delightful way to experiment with cross-stitches and since I considered it contemporary, I was not limited to the use of muted shades. With the help of bright colors, the stitches become more prominent.

Cross-stitches take very little concentration once the stitch unit is developed, and there is no distortion of canvas when using cross-stitch patterns. Just remember all the top stitches of the crosses must go in one direction.

The two kinds of crosses used in canvas embroidery are the diagonal cross and the **Upright Cross**.

UPRIGHT CROSS
(Straight Cross)

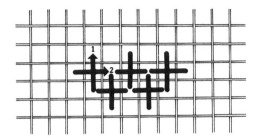

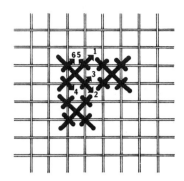

A cross-stitch that does not look like a cross-stitch at all, the Upright Cross has little horizontal nubs, which give it a very tweedy and tailored look. It takes shading well, and if worked in two colors, it has even more style. When worked over two threads, it covers the canvas well, which is surprising since the arms are vertical and horizontal. Of course, it is successful only when used with the proper ply yarn to the proper size canvas mesh—in this case it is 2-ply yarn on #12 threads to the inch mesh. It is also very important that all horizontal stitches are on the top. Otherwise, the texture is lost.

In the second row and all following rows, the stitches must fit up between the crosses of the first row, so that the vertical cross fits into the same hole as the horizontal cross.

Like most cross-stitches, the Upright Cross is amazingly simple to work, considering its impressive results. Perhaps these stitches have been slow in gaining popularity because each unit must be finished before going on to the next and there is no rhythmical swing to working the stitch.

RICE
(William & Mary, Crossed Corners)

The choice of what name to call this stitch is yours, but the logical one is Crossed Corners, because the stitch is a diagonal cross with each of its four corners crossed by another angle stitch forming another cross. It probably picked up the name **Rice** because of its Chinese origin, but that is only a guess. Two-ply Persian yarn is used for the large cross, and 1-ply for the angle stitch covering the tip of the arms.

It was not until the reign of William and Mary in the seventeenth century that the stitch became popular in England. Mary was a born needlewoman and made a diligent effort to become the patron saint of needlework. It was during her reign that the fully upholstered chair done in needlepoint came into vogue. It is said that her decoration of Hampton Court, that lovely palace surrounded by magnificent gardens, was one large flowered needlework design. To her we owe this pretty rosebud-like stitch.

The Rice stitch covers the canvas well and makes a stalwart but charming piece of upholstery upon completion. Covering a large area with it would be a lengthy project, however, as it is slow to work. Since the backing is firm and full, for small areas in the detail of a rug, it would be both durable and beautiful. It is at its best when two colors or two shades of one color are used.

Start at upper left and make a diagonal cross covering 2 threads. Cover the tip of each arm with a Tent stitch or a reversed Tent stitch, whichever the case may be.

Left-handed workers should start at lower left and at top of the stitch.

UPRIGHT CROSSED CORNERS

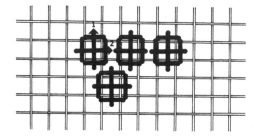

Using 2-ply Persian yarn for the large upright cross and 1-ply for the small stitches at the arm tips, here is another form of Crossed Corners. This can be done with one upright cross covering 2 threads and with single horizontal and vertical stitches covering the tips of the arms. It is best worked in units, and it is lost unless the tip stitches are done in another color.

Left-handed workers should start at lower left and at top of the stitch.

SMYRNA CROSS, DOUBLE STRAIGHT CROSS

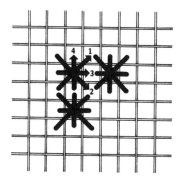

In the decorating trade a Smyrna is a domestic rug named after a city in Turkey; in canvas embroidery it is a stitch of great beauty. It is lovely for detail. Although frequently used for background, its effect is very pebbly. If a raised texture is desired, this is the stitch to

choose. It would be very effective for block lettering, because each unit forms a popcorn-like square. It is durable and covers the canvas well when worked with 2-ply Persian yarn.

The **Smyrna Cross** is simply two cross-stitches placed one atop the other. The bottom stitch is a diagonal cross-stitch, and the top one an upright one. The reverse is the **Double Straight Cross** where the upright is on the bottom. The crosses must cover two threads or multiples of two, and each should be completed before going on to the next. All crosses should overlap in the same direction. Two colors may be used if desired, but the stitches are dressy enough without more embellishment.

STAGGERED CROSS

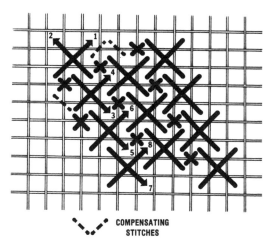

COMPENSATING STITCHES

A large and a small cross-stitch worked on a very gradual decline create an unusual texture. The diagram is deceiving because in form **Staggered Cross** looks like just any other large and small cross, but by the slightest deviation of the placement of the stitches, the result has the look of a rugged Scotch tweed. Two-ply yarn is used for both large and small crosses. It is difficult to recommend this for anything other than a background stitch. If the small stitch is worked in a contrasting color, it makes the pattern even more tweedy.

Starting at the top left, make the large diagonal cross over 2 threads. The descent is made by working the subsequent crosses on a staggered diagonal. The next large cross is started on the same line as the bottom of the first cross but 1 vertical thread over to the left. Continue this staggered decline diagonally down the canvas. The little crosses start 1 thread below and 1 thread to the left of the top left arm of the large cross and cover only one intersection. A routine path of execution is difficult to map out. Compensating stitches are necessary in any boundary area. They should be either a small cross worked over 1 thread or a Tent stitch worked from right to left or left to right, whichever the pattern dictates. All the top stitches of the cross should be made in the same direction.

Left-handed workers should start at lower left.

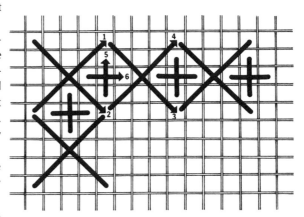

LARGE WITH UPRIGHT CROSS

This good-looking pattern consists of a rather large diagonal cross filled in with an upright cross giving the effect of a series of diamonds filled with a small nubbin. Since the combination of the large cross and the upright cross does not cover the canvas too well, either heavy yarn should be used or the background should be painted. It really makes quite a charming design and looks like a calico print when worked in two colors. By using 3-ply wool for the large cross and cotton or silk for the small cross, it becomes quite dressy. It is recommended for large areas but not for rugs because the large cross would easily snag.

The pattern of **Large with Upright Cross** consists of adjoining diagonal crosses going over 4 thread intersections and upright crosses going over 2. The upright crosses fill in the area left by the arms of the large cross. It is best to work all the large crosses in a horizontal row and then fill in with the small crosses. Compensating stitches for other than a straight or diagonal edge would be quite complicated. For the straight edge, use half of the upright cross making a vertical stitch over 2 threads and a horizontal stitch over 1 stitch. For the diagonal edge, make a vertical stitch over 1 thread and a horizontal thread over 1 thread.

Left-handed workers should start at lower left.

Doorstop

St. George & St. Andrew, Sheaf Stitches

A builder's brick covered with a pattern of needlepoint makes a distinctive doorstop. It is done on #10 canvas threads to the inch, with 3-ply Persian yarn. I searched for a stitch that would effectively simulate the cubed look of skyscrapers: a square stitch pattern with small holes in it to look like windows. It wasn't hard to find because cross-stitch patterns have to have a filler of some kind. The stitch called **St. George & St. Andrew** was perfect. It is a companion cross-stitch; St. George is a straight cross, and St. Andrew is a diagonal. The St. Andrew cross stands out a little bolder than the St. George. In the picture, it is the one with the lights on. This was the exact fenestration look I wanted. This is a very easy stitch to master and when used with the proper weight yarn, it covers the canvas well. It is even more charming when used in two colors.

During the Elizabethan period, England and Scotland were caught up in a whirl of needlepoint, and we well remember the rivalry between the two queen cousins, both ardent needlewomen, Elizabeth and Mary, Queen of Scots. The cross-stitch, long a favorite in European countries, started to gain popularity at this time, and it is very probable that the patron saints of England and Scotland found themselves companions on canvas if not on religious matters.

Color choice for the buildings was confined to subdued colors—two shades of gray and two shades of blue—because some parts of the building should be in shade. Rusts, light pink, and orange were used for the buildings reflecting the light. The promenade around the park seemed to cry out for something regimented and well kept—a cry heard loud and clear in most cities. The **Sheaf,** also known as the Shell stitch, is one of the bundle stitches, so named because several stitches are worked in a bunch and then tied together with a tie stitch. One sees this motif in Egyptian wall painting and embroidery. Early Egyptian homes were fenced with rows of bundles of wheat, or maize, symbolizing well-being. When it

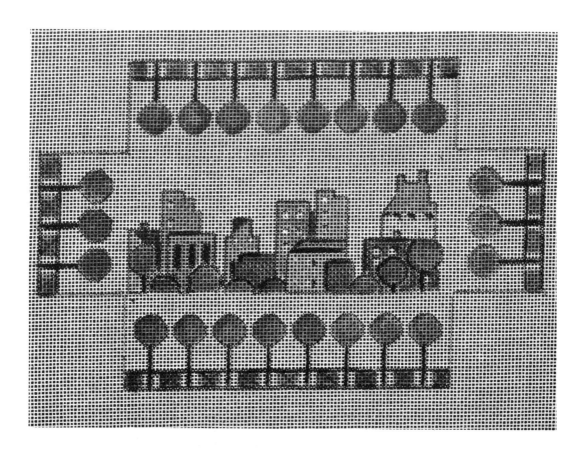

became an art motif, it was usually used as a border design or frieze. It is best suited as a border in canvas embroidery, too. While it requires some manipulation to tie up the bundles, it goes fast as it covers many threads in one stitch unit, and it is very decorative. Involving three different stitches to make one stitch unit, it affords the worker a chance to use three colors. The colors I used were chosen for their fresh brilliance: clear spring greens and yellow.

After creating this landscape of stitches and color, the choice of a background color became a real problem. A sky blue was too intense for the blue-gray of the buildings; the old faithful background

St. George & St. Andrew, Sheaf

beige did nothing; the bright park greens turned all other greens to mud. Obviously this should have been planned in advance. An orange-sherbet shade, one that seemed least likely to succeed, turned out to be the color most suitable to set off the buildings as well as to complement the trees and park. It gave an aura of sunset, and those lights were turned on just at the right time. What could have been a disaster became a pleasing combination of color. Though there are many hundreds of yarn colors from which to choose, there is never the luxury of the painter's pallette, and I learned through this experience to work out the background color while choosing the color of the design.

ST. GEORGE & ST. ANDREW

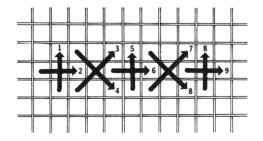

A combination of the Diagonal Cross and the Straight Cross alternating in horizontal rows constitute this stitch pattern. Make an upright cross over 2 threads and next to it make a diagonal cross over 2 threads and repeat these across the area to be covered. In the next row reverse the series. If using two colors, leave 2 canvas threads between stitches and complete all stitches of one type of cross, then return to fill in the spaces with the other cross. With an upright cross there is always the possibility of canvas showing, so it may be necessary to use a heavier yarn with this stitch.

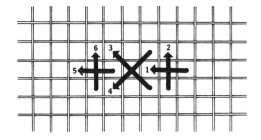

Left-handed workers would start at lower left of work for both the St. George and St. Andrew crosses. For the Straight Cross, the stitch would start at the top of the stitch unit.

SHEAF (SHELL)

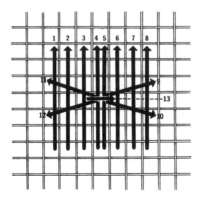

Since this stitch pattern covers never less than 4 vertical stitches in one stitch unit, it requires yarn weight that will cover the canvas well. Make 8 vertical stitches in a row, covering 6 canvas threads with stitches number 4 and 5 occupying the same holes. Bring needle out in the center of these stitches which will be between stitches #4 and #5. Make a slanting stitch to the right by putting the needle in 1 thread up and 3 threads over. Come back to center and make another slanted stitch going down 1 thread and 3 threads over. This sheaves half the bundle. Repeat these slanted stitches on the left side, and the harvesting is complete.

CROSS-STITCH ADDRESS BOOK

From top left, common cross stitch *(red box)*, Smyrna *(yellow)*, Rice *(blue)*, Upright *(beige)*, Upright Crossed Corners *(yellow-green)*, Staggered *(rust)*, Large with Upright *(dark-red)*, Double Straight *(gray)*

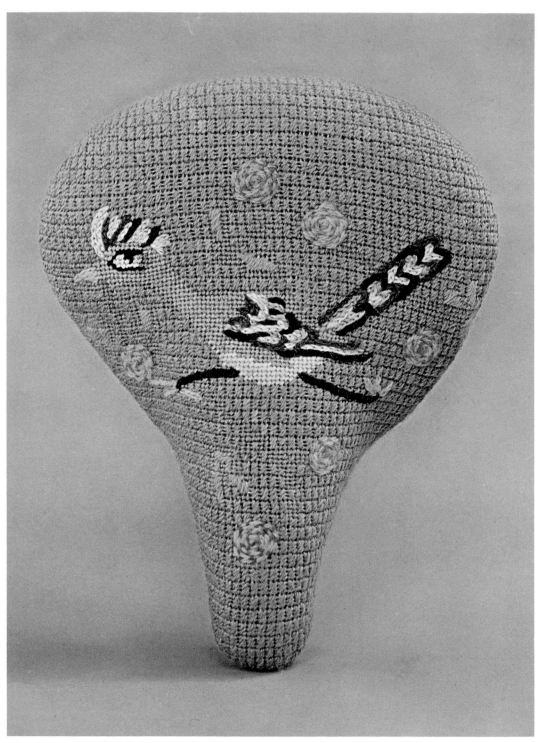

BICYCLE-SEAT COVER

Bicycle-Seat Cover

Cashmere, Chain, Tent Circular Couching, Satin Stitches

Needlepoint can be pedaled around town on a bicycle. It need not be confined to the sanctity of four walls, for it is so durable that it can withstand the rigors of sea and land. Many a cabin cruiser and sailboat sport handworked canvas embroidery on deck, in the cabin, and on the captain, be it as pillows, binnacle cover, or belt. There are also many devices made of needlepoint to be found on the golf course, and on the tennis court. For the disciple of the bicycle, there is a seat cover. The design is worked on #12 canvas threads to the inch with 2-ply Persian yarn. The pattern used for the seat itself may have to be adjusted in size to fit a particular model.

This two-wheeling accessory must be made strong and durable to withstand inclement as well as sunny weather, so the choice of a background stitch is important. An upright stitch would not be recommended, but there are many good angle background stitches that are sturdy. We want an angle stitch that moves along swiftly, too, because a bike seat should not be a lifelong project. If worked in one of the checkered stitches such as the Mosaic, Scotch, or Cashmere, the seat will have durability.

The **Cashmere** stitch is used in this project for the background. It wears well and will outlast any bicycle, let alone rider. It is effortless to do, a fast moving stitch unit that is made up of 2 single Tent stitches and 2 elongated angle stitches forming a rectangle. Cashmere covers the canvas well, and when worked, it makes a pattern of diagonal lines to form a twill-like weave. Its pattern forms a soft pile not found in the more restricted stitches; in short, it makes a comfy seat. The canvas is stretched out of shape only moderately, and the looseness of the two elongated stitches make it easy to block.

The design on this seat is a roadrunner, appropriately tearing along with complete abandon. It has rather delicate shading in browns and tans, and could easily become an extensive piece of needlework if worked in small definitive stitches, but as your bicycle accessory might be pinched in the supermarket parking lot, perhaps a less ambitious stitch should be used. The versatile **Chain** stitch, one of the loop stitches, is a whiz of a stitch that can be worked in any direction—around curves, up and down, and on angles—and takes no time at all to cover the canvas in a very pleasant way. It also has a feather-like smoothness and, in this case, was chosen to add interest to the bird's tail, wings, and crest.

The rest of the roadrunner is done in the **Tent** stitch. With the texture of the background stitch so visibly patterned, the evenness of the Tent stitch attracts more attention to the bird than if it were stitched in elaborate raised work. The smooth surface against the rough surface creates a contrast that complements both textures.

The flowers are done in the **Circular Couching** stitch that swirls around in lollipop fashion, with a series of overcast stitches that anchor an underlay of yarn to the canvas. It is often thought of as a surface stitch only, but it is easily adapted to canvas embroidery. In the previous project, it is worked in three directions, but here it is used in a circular form.

The leaves are done in the **Satin** stitch, a simple over-and-over stitch worked on a diagonal. Both the Couching and Satin stitches are best used for small details because several threads of canvas are covered in one laid stitch and would not be durable for large areas. The stitches are flat and smooth and hug the canvas well.

Selecting colors is purely a matter of preference in this design. The background color should naturally be practical. Charcoal gray, brown, or blue or a

Circular Couching (flower), *Satin* (leaf), *Chain* (plumage), *Cashmere* (background)

bottle green are good colors that can withstand the elements.

Strangely enough, the stitches selected for this piece are all related to handwork done in India, and all are of ancient origin. Originally cashmere was a soft woolen fabric woven in India from the long fine undercoat of the Kashmir goat. During the mid-eighteenth century, England and Scotland started producing a soft dress fabric from the fleece of the very popular merino sheep and they called *this* cashmere. It had a soft twill weave and was woven in such a way that there were distinct diagonal lines going across the fabric. The Cashmere needlepoint stitch resembles this twill. There are variations of the stitch that are similar in structure, such as the Oriental and the

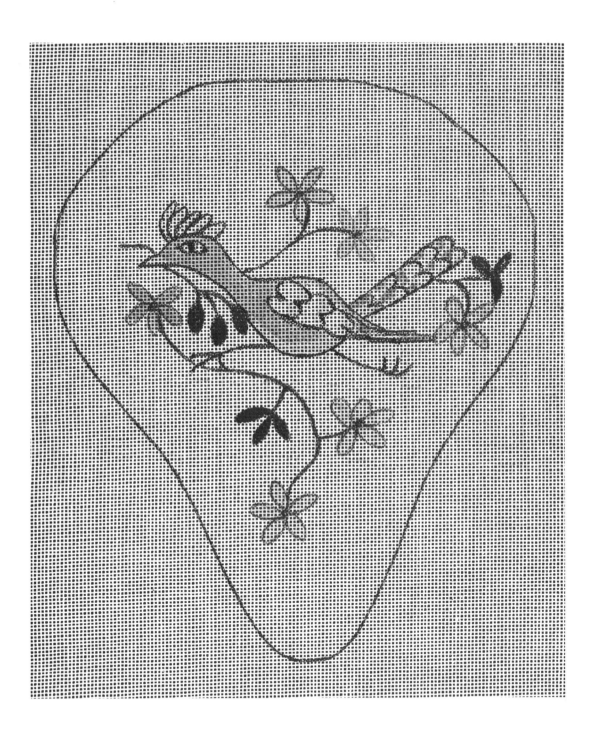

Mosaic, but neither makes a twill pattern. The Cashmere, like its variations, is most often used in large areas for background, because its charm lies in its all-over textured effect, but it can also make a nice trim border stitch for a bold design.

The Chain stitch is one of the oldest surviving stitches. The Hermitage Museum in Leningrad has some pieces of cloth with the Chain stitch that date back to the fifth century B.C. Today exquisite work is done in this stitch in the Punjab area of India. When worked with a needle, it is called the Chain stitch, but when worked with a hook (which then requires a drumlike hoop called a tambour) it becomes the Tambour stitch. It forms a series of loops connecting in a coupling fashion like railroad cars, and at one time it was even called the Railway stitch.

The Satin stitch is worked beautifully in gold silk on muslin in the Bengal section of India. It was introduced to this country by the Moravians from Germany; they usually worked it on a satin ground with satin thread, which lent itself well to their popular hearts-and-flowers scenes and from whence it got its name.

CASHMERE

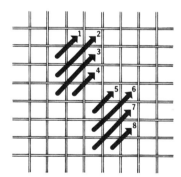

The series of rectangles that form a Cashmere stitch pattern may be worked on a diagonal, or they may be worked up and down the canvas or across in straight rows. When worked diagonally, it is easier to get into a speedy rhythm because the stitches fall easily into place from one box to another. However, this diagonal pull of the stitches causes a slight lopsided distortion of the canvas. Starting at upper left, make a simple Tent stitch, come out 1 hole below the base of the first stitch. Angle the next stitch over 2 horizontal canvas threads and 2 vertical threads, reaching the same top level as the first Tent stitch. Come out again 1 hole below the last elongated Tent stitch and repeat this stitch again. Make a fourth Tent stitch to conclude the rectangular box formation. Repeat this box in adjacent positions, either diagonally, vertically, or horizontally.

Left-handed workers start from the bottom left of the piece and work to the right and up.

CHAIN

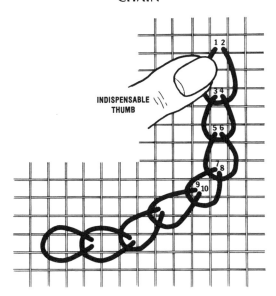

CIRCULAR COUCHING

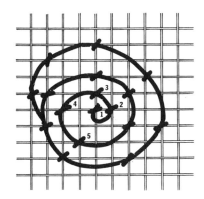

Start from the inside in escargot fashion and, as if coiling lines aboard ship, wind the yarn on the surface to make a continuously enlarging circle, securing the yarn in as regular intervals as necessary with a Tent stitch. End the coil by inserting the yarn from the coil through the canvas, and secure.

SATIN

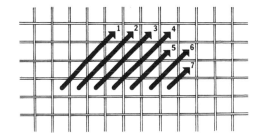

Loop stitches, such as the Chain stitch and the Buttonhole stitch, require the use of the guiding thumb of the left hand, or in the case of left-handers, the thumb of the right hand. The needle must go through a loop, and without the help of the thumb as an anchor and guide for the loop, it would be like trying to spear a fish. Starting at the top of the area to be outlined, bring the needle out from the back and make a loop by inserting the needle in the same hole. Hold the loop with the thumb and bring the needle out 3 horizontal threads below and through the captured loop. Make another loop, again going into the same hole you just came out, anchoring the loop with the thumb until secured by the next chain link. And so it goes, curving and swooping around as smoothly as a car on the Indianapolis raceway.

Make a parallel series of slanting stitches going over 2 or more horizontal threads, as the shape of the design indicates.

Barn-Owl Picture

Couching Stitches—Horizontal, Vertical, and Diagonal

This is a cute little owl and could be done entirely in the Tent stitch without additional embellishment and still be as saucy as intended. However, in this project he is going to be used as a picture, and texture as well as color can help the features carry farther across the room. So we will give him a little preening. He is worked on #12 canvas threads to the inch with 2-ply Persian yarn for the long under stitches and 1 single strand for the overlay stitch.

Stitches that form a smooth texture similar to the plumage of our feathered friends would be the first candidates for selection. A bird's feathers seem to follow the contours of the bird's body, so that stitches capable of going in more than one direction would be appealing. The Gobelin stitches could qualify, but they should be saved for areas requiring delicate shading, so I settled on the **Couching** stitches.

The Couching stitches have a flat stitch (a laid stitch) with an overlay stitch (Couching stitch) that adds texture. They can be worked in any direction, so off we go making ruffled feathers. I chose barn-owl colors of beiges and brown with a lighter color for the breast and with gray blue for the background, to look like barn siding. Stripes were added to give a clapboard effect using two lines of darker shades of the gray blue. (I learned later that the boards on old barns were usually laid vertically rather than horizontally so my notions of clapboard were wrong.) The background is done in the Tent stitch to keep the surface flat and to bring out the contrasting texture of the bird.

Now, where to use the various couching stitches? The bars on the breast of the owl were done in a series of **Horizontal Couching** units covering 4 threads with an overlay of angle stitches in a darker color. This overlay gives the effect of the bars while the underthread gives the smoothness of the feathered breast. The **Vertical Couching** stitches on the wings of the owl follow the elongated feathered wing units portrayed in the design,

as well as following the contour of the body. The eye of the owl was done in **Diagonal Couching** to give it the not quite centered, icy look we associate with this bird of prey. The smoothness of this stitch also adds to the effect.

The Couching stitch is just a long stitch tied down by a short stitch. If it covers more than 12 threads, however, the stitch may become a little wavy. As I have already mentioned, it may go horizontally, vertically, or diagonally. It may also go around in a circle. (This circle stitch unit is used as a flower in the Bicy-

Couching stitches: Diagonal (eyes), *Horizontal* (breast), *Vertical* (wings)

cle-Seat Cover project on page 49.) The tying-down or short overlay stitches may also be worked as horizontal, vertical, or diagonal stitches. They may be worked as close as 2 threads apart or as far apart as 4 to 6 threads, depending upon the durability desired from the stitch. The nearer the overlay stitches are placed, the less the chance that the long stitch will snag. These overlay stitches look best evenly spaced.

Couching is often found in fine embroidery and is best used in small intricate areas where its smoothness and delicacy can be appreciated. In early embroidery circles it was known as the Tied stitch, and examples are found on work done in the fifteenth century, though its history may go back many centuries more. Couching is also referred to as the Roman stitch or Roumanian Couching.

HORIZONTAL COUCHING

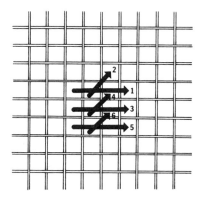

From left to right, make a fairly loose horizontal stitch covering 3 canvas threads. Go back 2 threads and tie it down with a slanting stitch covering one intersection. If couching over 6 to 9 canvas threads, 2 or 3 evenly spaced slanting stitches are required for the tie-down. An upright stitch may be used in place of the slanting stitch.

Left-handed workers should start from right to left. The overlay stitches start at the top and go down and over.

VERTICAL COUCHING

From bottom to top, make a long stitch covering 8 canvas threads vertically. Back up 2 horizontal threads and make a slanting stitch. Back up 2 horizontal threads and make a second slanting stitch. Back up 2 more threads and make another slanting stitch. This will show you how to space your tie-down stitches evenly. The use of a darker or lighter shade, or even a different color, for the overlay stitch makes a very interesting pattern. The overlay stitches may be staggered from row to row, so that they will not all be directly across from

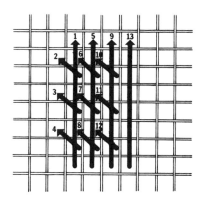

the former row. Many combinations and different arrangements are possible.

Left-handed workers should follow the same procedure as in Horizontal Couching.

DIAGONAL COUCHING

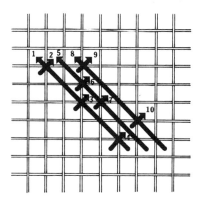

Make a slanting stitch on a true diagonal covering 5 threads of canvas from right to left. Back up 1 thread, make a slanting stitch. Back up 2 threads, make another slanting stitch. If staggering the tie-down, back up 2 threads first. Continue this tie-down along the diagonal rows.

Left-handed workers should start at top right and go down to the left. Overlay stitches are made from left to right going down.

Bordered Handbag

**Reverse Side Basket Weave, Herringbone, Tent, Long-Armed Cross,
Double Straight Cross, Van Dyke Stitches**

A prefab handbag offers an ideal opportunity for a decorative needlepoint border or an appliqué, and can make something ordinary into a beautiful accessory. In this project a border of needlepoint was appliquéd to the bottom rim of a cylindrical-shaped purse. Try to find a handbag in a solid color with a single seam at the back rather than one at each side so that matching the seam of the purse to the end seam of the needlepoint border can be done in one operation. A seam in needlepoint does not mesh with the ease of a zipper.

This particular bag is covered in an interesting fabric resembling a basket-weave homespun pattern, but any sturdy fabric that will hold a firm stitch for the appliqué will do. We have all admired the interesting reverse side of our Diagonal Tent or Basket Weave stitches and bewailed the fact that no one would see it. So with the close match of the bag fabric to the weave of the **Reverse Side Basket Weave** stitch, it seemed the opportune occasion to work the reverse

side as the front side. It was something I had wanted to do for a long time. The stitches are done on #12 canvas threads to the inch with 2-ply Persian yarn. Working from the back side, at first I did a lot of peeking to see if all was going well on the front, and it was—until I got to the area around the design. Then after much rear viewing, I finally turned the canvas to the front and used a plucking method, a two-motion stitch, to make the proper interweaving. I chose the same sand color as the handbag fabric, which was well suited to the design since sandpipers are usually seen scurrying around sand flats.

Although there was no indication of water in the original design, by using **Herringbone,** a bold conspicuous stitch, I created a fairly turbulent sea in the background, thereby relieving the monotony of the smoothness of the sand. The Herringbone is an interlacing cross-stitch of great strength and durability, sometimes known as the Interlacing stitch. It is often used for rugs as well as for borders on

large pieces of canvas embroidery. The stitch forms a path like the imprint left by skiers going uphill. Giotto, who was far removed from the ski slopes in both age and interest, painted the Herringbone stitch in the borders of clothing on some of his figures to enhance the composition of his work. It can be seen on the gold border of the robe worn by the figure in the foreground in the "Last Supper" at the Arena Chapel in Padua, painted by Giotto at the beginning of the fourteeenth century. Upon close examination, the stitch has been copied so precisely that it is not inconceivable to think that the painter himself may have taken up embroidery before executing it.

Sandpipers scoot along the edge of the waves at quite a clip, so I have never determined their exact color, but my impression is of black and gray with white

markings. The combination of the bird and sand colors is so wonderful that I feel that it must be one of those lovely color contrivances of nature and not just a casual association that turned out well.

With the exception of the wing feathers and the eyes, the plumage of the sandpipers is done in the **Tent** stitch. The wing feathers, a warm gray in color, are done in the **Long-Armed Cross** or Long-Legged Cross stitch, with a stripe of white Tent stitch between the bars. Arms or legs, they are both the same stitch, and as the name indicates, the cross has one arm longer than the other, actually double in length. This extended arm gives the row of stitches a long smooth look, far more beautiful than the square boxlike unit that one associates with the plain Cross. It is similar to the Herringbone to execute, but in appearance it is far more sleek and smooth and resembles a beautiful piece of satin braid. A very versatile stitch, it can be worked on the diagonal, as well as the horizontal and vertical, which the wing feathers of two of the sandpipers require.

The origin of this stitch is reported to be Moorish, and it has been particularly prevalent in the embroidery motifs of Morocco and Portugal. These two countries, separated by the narrowest of passages, are miles apart in cultural similarities yet cling to the same embroidery stitches introduced to them centuries ago. Though they may lay claim to the stitch, "the Greeks have a word for it": the Greek Cross stitch. Its popularity may lie in its economy as well as its beauty. For the amount of area covered, it uses very little yarn, is very compact, and covers the canvas well. Its neat appearance may also influence people to use it in both utilitarian and decorative work.

The eyes of the birds are done in the **Double Straight Cross.** Despite its conflicting name, when used singly as an accent, it is a pretty little stitch, and when used as a background or in large areas it resembles the fine crochet of the Pop-

Double Straight Cross (eye), *Herringbone* (wings), *Van Dyke* (grass), *Reverse Side Basket Weave* (background)

corn stitch so popular in the mid-nineteenth century.

The almost imperceptible leaf stitch is called the **Van Dyke** after the seventeenth-century Flemish painter. It makes the lacelike edging that can be seen in his portraits. This is purely a surface stitch and the only one in our bag. It does not cover the canvas as a unit nor will its rays mesh when used in a row. I worked it with a single strand of yarn. It creates a feathery effect, and the distinct center vein simulates the stiffness of fine marsh grass.

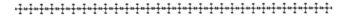

REVERSE SIDE BASKET WEAVE

Follow the directions for the Basket Weave stitch on page 30, using the reverse side as the front. The beginning and ending of thread are done on the front side of the regular Basket Weave stitch.

VAN DYKE

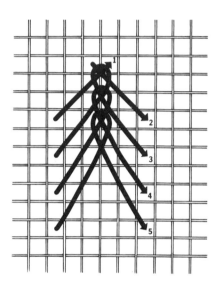

Bring needle out 3 threads down and 3 threads to the left of area to be covered. Put needle in to the right 3 threads up and 3 threads over. Next bring needle out 1 thread to the left and put needle in 3 threads down and 3 threads to the right. This makes an elongated cross. The next stitches vary from the first unit. Bring needle out 2 threads below of start of first stitch unit. Instead of making a cross by bringing needle out 1 thread to the left at top of cross, pass the needle *under* the crossed stitches of the first unit but do not penetrate the canvas. Complete stitch by inserting the needle in 3 threads to the right and down 3 threads. Continue following stitches in a vertical row in the same manner as the second stitch.

Left-handed workers should bring needle

out 3 threads down and 3 threads to the right of area to be covered. Then continue to follow the directions above, reversing "left" and "right."

LONG-ARMED CROSS

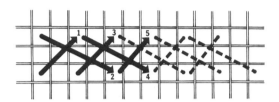

Work from left to right. Start at the bottom left of the cross to be made, going up 2 horizontal threads and over 2 vertical threads. This is the short arm. Bring needle out 2 threads to the left. Make another stitch 2 threads down and 4 threads over. This is the long arm. Come out 2 threads to the left. Repeat these two crosses. Both crosses, long and short, seek the same level at the top and bottom of the row.

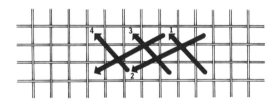

Left-handed workers should start at the lower right and work across the canvas to the left.

DOUBLE STRAIGHT CROSS

Not as sinister a stitch as it sounds, this is merely an upright cross and in this project covering 4 threads vertically and 4 threads horizontally with a smaller diagonal cross overlay. For further directions see page 108.

HERRINGBONE

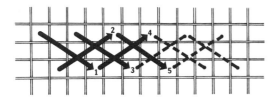

This stitch is best done horizontally. It is mostly executed on the surface, so the reverse side shows only a tiny running stitch. Work all rows from left to right. Starting the first cross at the top, make the under arm by going over 3 vertical threads and down 2 horizontal threads. Bring the needle out 2 threads to the left and complete the top arm of the cross by going up over 3 vertical and up 2 horizontal threads. This brings you up to the level of the top of the under cross arm. Start the next cross by coming out 2 stitches to the left and then follow the directions of the first cross. This really becomes a swinging stitch, and it is disappointing when the rhythm is interrupted and the row comes to an end.

Left-handed workers should start the rows from the bottom right, working across to the left of the canvas.

Bargello Pillow

Bargello Scallop

Bargello (pronounced Bar-jello) is a good introduction to the upright stitches. It is a simple stitch crossing over a specified number of horizontal threads, usually 2 to 6, as the design indicates, and making a fabric-like pattern. In most Bargello patterns, particularly those called Flame patterns, all rows paralleling the first design row are identical. When the first row is started in the center, the following

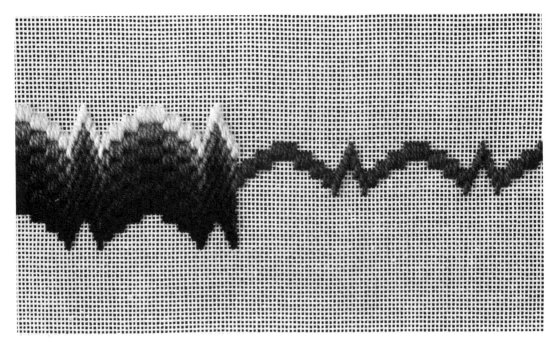

BARGELLO PICTURE FRAME

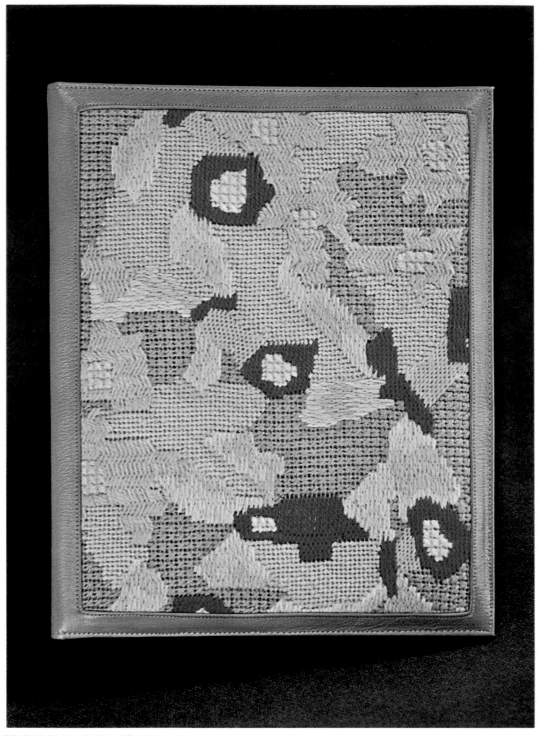

TELEPHONE-BOOK COVER

rows may be worked toward either the bottom or the top of the piece. When the first row is started at the top, it may be continued down to the border of the proportions desired. The stitch is easy to learn and enjoyable to do and goes like the wind once a rhythm is established. I nearly completed a fair sized pillow (my first, and of the pattern illustrated) in thirteen hours while waiting for a plane in the Moscow airport. When used on #13 or #14 canvas threads to the inch, it covers the canvas threads well for an upright stitch.

The Bargello pillow illustrated was done on #14 canvas threads to the inch with 3-ply Persian yarn. This particular **Bargello Scallop** pattern is one of the easiest to work. I used five shades of one color with each row worked in one shade. Color and speed explain the fascination of these stitch patterns, but color is the key. They can be worked monochromatically as in the example or in a combination of colors. Color combinations that you would never think of as compatible become a delightful surprise. Oranges and purples, pinks and reds, when subtly shaded, blend as nicely as a pousse-café and look as if they tasted as good. Do remember, however, that the charm of Bargello lies in the subtle gradation of several shades of one or more colors forming undulating areas of dark to light, rather than a series of unrelated colors worked into a labyrinth.

It is said that the Bargello stitch originated in the sixteenth century in the prison in Florence, Italy, from which it got its name. It is odd to think of the Bargello stitch starting life behind bars, for it is the most free and uninhibited of stitches.

Bargello Scallop

The Moors, those creative invaders from North Africa, are also credited with having brought the stitch to Spain, from whence it spread through the continent of Europe. But whatever its origin, the popularity of the Bargello stitch has swept across the needlepoint world the way the waves of its stitches sweep across the canvas, and it has been popular in every period of modern needlepoint history. By the eighteenth century, the beginning of American affluence, it had reached American shores and was referred to as the "Flame stitch." There are a number of pieces of antique furniture seen in museums today that still retain their original covers done in Bargello. These heirlooms have a beautiful muted coloration that makes us think that our forebears were highly subdued in their taste. We must take into account, however, that the dyes, particularly the

66   BARGELLO PILLOW

reds and blues, have faded perceptibly over the the years and that these quiet, dignified pieces were once as bright as a kiosk. Today, with our potpourri of modern and traditional furnishings, the Bargello patterns fit into any decor.

A number of our creative modern needlework designers have devised many unusual and stunning patterns of medallions and chevrons which follow the technique of the old motif, while embellishing it. Plotting the course of the series of waves in Flame patterns is far easier than it looks. There are two ways to set up the design. The first is to find the center of the piece you intend to copy and the center of your canvas. If there is no ruler handy, an easy way to find the middle of the canvas is to fold it in half and mark the approximate center, and then fold it in half the other way and mark the approximate center again. Follow these marks until they meet, and behold, that is the center. Next, make a first stitch in the center, corresponding to the center of your design copy, covering the prescribed number of horizontal threads you must cross. From the center, follow the pattern in a horizontal row first to the right and then to the left.

The second way to set up the design is to start from a boundary edge and work horizontally until you reach a satisfactory width, ending the row with the pattern corresponding to the beginning of the row. This method is naturally less reliable and accurate if a definite size is required.

This is, of course, the simplest of patterns. By varying the number of consecutive threads worked horizontally or the length of the stitches, all kinds of elaborate scallops and geometric designs result. There is no end to the variations of line and color that can be used in creating a Bargello pattern.

If you select a pattern with a unit of design like a medallion, also find the center of the canvas and the center of the pattern and copy one unit completely. Then extend a single row from the completed unit to both the right and the left to establish a basic line pattern from which all consecutive rows will follow. By finishing an entire unit, you have a much better idea of what the groundwork ahead will look like. But even so, there is always a fascinating element of surprise right down to the last row in doing Bargello.

Even though this stitch is so elementary, merely a vertical stitch covering from 2 to 6 horizontal threads, there are a few helpful hints that make it simpler to work. The very first stitch is hard to secure and can loosen easily. Hold the end of the thread in the back of the canvas tightly until it is well worked into the following stitches. This helps to keep it firm. Vertical stitches do not cover as well as angle stitches, so for all Bargello either use a heavier yarn or a mesh with more threads (smaller holes) per inch. Even when using a 3-ply Persian yarn, use a canvas mesh with smaller holes than you would normally. Fourteen threads to the inch is satisfactory, and 13 threads, if available, is ideal. Do not pull your stitches too tight, because the canvas threads will then bunch up, distorting the canvas weave, and the result will be an uneven stitch. A tight stitch also causes an ugly gap between the rows of stitches. There is always a small gap between rows that is unavoidable, but it can be controlled by keeping the stitches loose.

There is a little-known flame stitch

called the Split Florentine in which one stitch is inserted through the bottom of the stitch in the preceding row making a woven effect like tapestry. It is similar to the Split Encroached Gobelin stitch (see page 92). Using the Split Florentine method will correct the gaping problem, but the result of this encroaching is a little on the fuzzy side. It lacks that neat regimented look of the Bargello, and this may account for its lack of popularity with Bargello workers.

BARGELLO SCALLOP

This pillow will measure 12 by 12 inches if worked on #14 canvas threads to the inch with 3-ply Persian yarn.

All the stitches in this design pattern cover 4 horizontal threads. It is a series of ascending and descending steps, forming a scallop. The steps are made into units, the number of stitches in each varying. Each successive unit of stitches in this pattern is 2 threads higher than the previous one when going up, and 2 threads lower when going down. The scallop starts with an ascending unit of 2, then 3, 4, 6, stitches. After the count of 6, the units start a descent of the same count, only reversed: 4, 3, 2, as it goes down the scallop, 2 stitches with each unit.

Each scallop is flanked by a V shape made of 5 stitches for the ascent and 4 for the descent. At that point the design is repeated, starting with the 2-stitch clump. At the end of the row change yarn color and proceed with the stitches following directly underneath and with the same count as in the preceding row.

Bargello Picture Frame

Bargello Stitch

This series of squares, each measuring 1½ inches, is done in the **Bargello** stitch on #14 canvas threads to the inch with 3-ply Persian yarn. The frame pattern is made on the diagonal so that this pattern of squares will leave an opening in the standard picture size of 5 by 7 inches. This is tricky to set up, but once the first square is counted out, the rest is clear sailing. Many frame patterns in Bargello or other stitches can be worked on the "straight" of the canvas and need not be drawn on a diagonal. However, when making up a pattern, be sure that the size of the opening will fit a standard-size picture.

To follow this particular design pattern, hold the canvas as you would normally and start the first box at the top left-hand corner of the frame. Think of the top half of the tipped square as a pitched roof and the bottom half as V-shaped. Make a stitch in the peak of the roof over 4 horizontal threads. From this center stitch, make 9 stitches over 4 threads descending one thread each stitch on the left-hand side of the roof; on the tenth stitch, continue the diagonal but shorten the stitches to cover 3 threads, then 2 threads, and then 1.

Bargello

See color picture opposite page 64   **69**

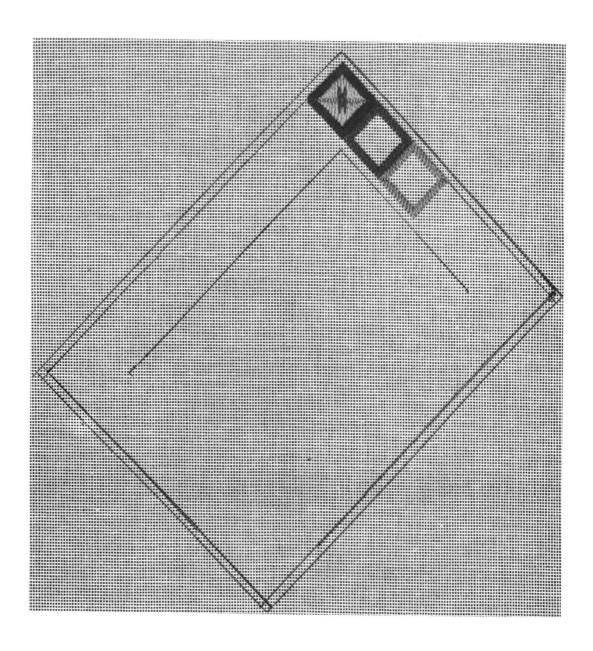

These decreasing stitches will be on a line with the bottom of stitch #9.

Start the V with a stitch over 1 thread directly under that of the last stitch of the left side of the roof. Make the next over 2 threads going down the side of the V, then over 3 threads, then over 4 threads for a total of 9 times. The tenth stitch will be the center stitch for the V and should be on a line with the center stitch of the roof. Repeat this count in reverse for the right-hand side of the V going up.

To fill in the roof, start at the left side going up on a diagonal with vertical stitches covering a sequence of 1, 2, 3, 4, 5, 6, 7, 4, 7 threads. The last "7" is a common stitch with the right side which will be repeated in reverse going down. To fill the center area of the V, start at the left with the same count going down and then reverse the count to go up. There will be an area left in the center for 3 stitches on each side.

The middle one of these three center stitches is a joint stitch that covers 4 threads, 2 of each triangle. The two flanking stitches cover 2 stitches on each side. These 3 center stitches must be done in a different color, or there is no reason for the filler count to be as it is.

Start the next square diagonally down from the first square.

The border, both inside and outside the squares, covers 4 vertical threads.

Medallion Pillow

Radial Bargello

If you are a Bargello fan, here is a variation that will take you off the straight and narrow path of working in long parallel lines and swing you into a world of beautiful kaleidoscopic forms. Using the same Bargello stitch, and dividing the canvas into four pie-shaped segments of identical size radiating from a central axis, you can duplicate a sunburst or starlike shape with the same ease and pleasure you do the regular Bargello patterns. You can even take a segment from one of your favorite Bargello patterns, and by centering it and then working it in four identical sections, you can make a formal symmetrical design like a paper cutout or an intricate lace doily. The pillow illustrated is done on #14 canvas threads to the inch with 3-ply Persian yarn. I used five shades of one color, but many delightful combinations and gradations of color may be used to make this and other exotic shapes.

To transfer a quadrilateral symmetrical design freehand onto needlepoint canvas is difficult, because you run the risk of making an error in counting that can completely throw off a rosette-type pattern. You can chart each stitch on graph paper and then duplicate the count on the canvas, but not many people can take this laborious process for very long. **Radial Bargello** is the answer. Working the Bargello stitch in quadrants will produce a geometric design with all four sections exactly alike. This method is as speedy as the straight Bargello and is even more fascinating.

With a long basting stitch or a tested waterproof pen, make two diagonal lines in the form of an X through the center of the canvas, dividing it into four equal parts. The canvas acts as graph paper, and a true diagonal can be easily followed. It is very important that these sectional guidelines or radial lines, as we shall call them, are on a *true diagonal* and that all four sections are exactly the same in size. Check and recheck each radial line because if they are off, the design will not come out the same on all four sides.

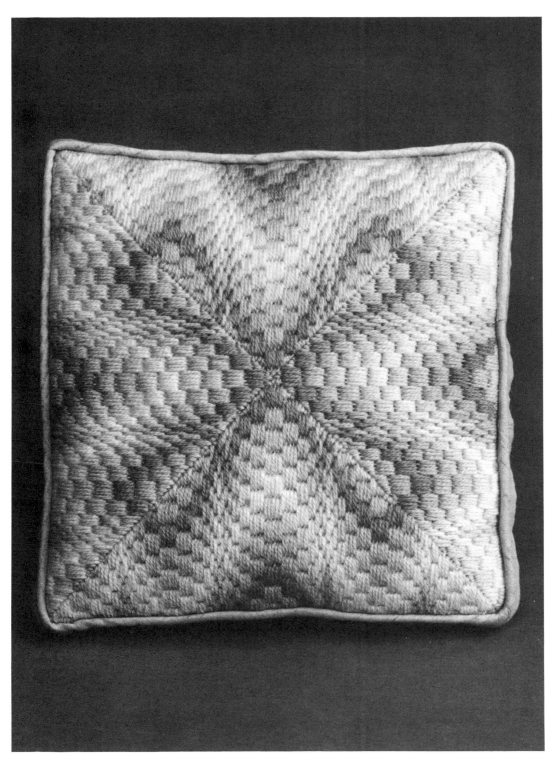

To start a pattern, with a piece of thread, make a line down the center of one of the quadrants, dividing it in half. Drop down about mid-center of this center line and make a stitch going over the number of threads required in the pattern you are doing (this example is over 6 threads), then continue with a row of stitches following a design of peaks or curves as in a regular Bargello pattern. Work first to the right over to the radial line and then to the left over to the other radial line to form the pattern row. This first pattern row will be the basis of your design and will be copied in all the other rows. The last stitch of the row at the end of each side of a quadrant unit must fit into the boundary of the radial line and in most cases will have to be graduated in length. In other words, the top of the last stitch of the row will hit the radial line and may stretch from 1 to 6 threads

in height. To finish the first quadrant, work the rows from the basic row inward to the center axis and outward to the boundary of the design.

Now swing the canvas around and repeat the same operation in the next quadrant section. Your stitches will be perpendicular or at right angles to the stitches of the first quadrant. The last stitch in each row will share the same hole as the end stitch of the corresponding row of each adjacent section. This is the key and the checkpoint for each section, and the top of the last stitch of the fourth quadrant will therefore fit into the same canvas hole as the top of the last stitch of the first quadrant.

The fun starts with the changes in color in each row as in regular Bargello when your pattern will start to resemble the most beautiful snowflake. While working in the same color yarn, it is possible to work the same row in all four quadrants by turning the canvas at the completion of each segment row. The

Radial Bargello

suspense of how the design is developing, however, will often hold you captive in one single section until it is completed.

As in regular Bargello, the use of either a canvas mesh with more threads to the inch or a heavier yarn is advised.

Phulkari Picture Frame

Phulkari Stitch

Phulkari (pronounced Pool-car-rhee) is a fascinating Indian embroidery stitch that has been adapted to canvas embroidery and is used here as a front panel of a picture frame. The frame I chose was a light-weight folding one (5 by 7 inches), covered in Chinese silk. It had probably been designed as a traveling frame, but with the addition of an appliquéd panel of needlepoint on the front, its traveling days were over, and it became a lovely appointment for a room.

Since I planned to make only the front panel, I wanted it to go well with the silk covering on the back. Because of the delicacy of the frame itself, a wool appliqué would have been too cumbersome, so a silk thread was used which, in texture, was similar to the silk on the back. Embroidery cotton would have given somewhat the same effect with a more highly polished gloss. French silk, which is quite expensive, comes in a multitude of related colors in skeins 9 feet long and in 7 strands. The full 7 strands were used on #16 threads to the inch mono-mesh.

Embroidery cotton would be used in full strength, too.

A highly textured stitch would be too heavy for this piece, so I was in search of a smooth damask-type stitch. Any of the Florentine or Bargello patterns would have been appropriate. The Hungarian stitch would have been good, too, but I was in quest of something new. I had seen a lovely embroidered temple hanging worked in a stitch called Phulkari on dark red cotton at the Pace Gallery in New York City. Then, in a magazine article I found the stitch featured as a canvas-embroidery stitch. It works up quickly into lovely patterns and is interesting to do. The stitch is too loose for rug use, but it could be used on chair seats or pillows or on any object where a Bargello stitch can be used.

Phulkari originates from the Punjab province of India, where this exquisite embroidery work is still done today. The Indian technique is to stitch the fabric from the back. Our adaptation, fortunately, is to stitch from the front, and I

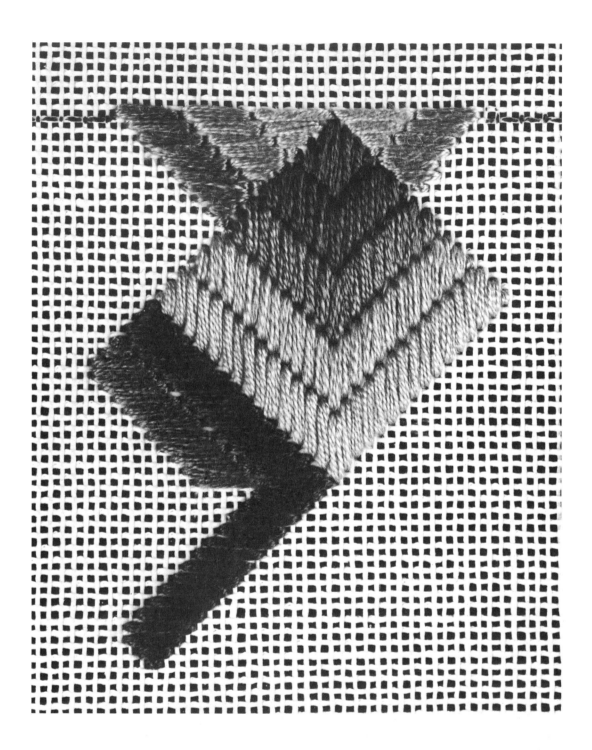

daresay it is a lot easier to work it on our graphlike mesh than on fine Indian cotton. Phulkari is a pattern that produces interesting lighting effects. I have seen it worked on canvas in one color of wool yarn, and when light strikes it from a certain direction, it will take on the subtle shading of two colors. The example shown is done in two closely related shades of one color. By altering the position of the frame to the light, its facets change into many different shades similar to the effect of a cut jewel. This shade variation is not only caused by the light and the sheen of the silk, but by the direction of the Phulkari stitches themselves. This illusive subtlety is fascinating.

Phulkari, like Bargello, requires only one kind of straight stitch to cover the canvas. It is worked in a series of large

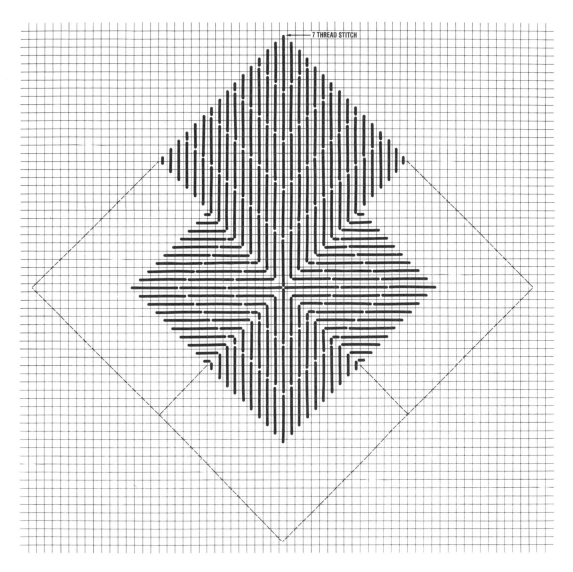

7 THREAD STITCH

diamond units each made up of a small top center diamond and 4 adjoining rows of chevrons, graduated in size, below it. These 4 chevrons and small diamond form a patterned unit and like a Radial Bargello design, the direction of the stitches of the neighboring diamond patterns will be changed from vertical to horizontal stitches, whichever the case may be.

At the top center of your canvas, make a stitch covering 7 horizontal threads. This is the only stitch in the entire diamond pattern unit that will span 7 threads. Drop down 1 thread to the right and make a stitch covering 5 horizontal threads. Drop down 1 thread to the right again and make a stitch covering 3 threads and then 1 thread. Repeat this on the other side of the 7-thread stitch, completing the little diamond.

The 4 chevron rows follow around the base of the small diamond with stitches covering 6 horizontal threads but grading off at each end of the row which will follow the count of the small diamond: 1, 3, 5, to start the chevron row from the left and 5, 3, 1, to end it. Complete the large diamond unit and then turn your canvas around 45° or a quarter of the way around and start another small diamond at the point of the broken line of the side of the first diamond.

When starting on a new pattern unit, as in all upright stitches, hold on to the first stitch from the back until it is firmly worked into the following stitches and well secured. Silk and cotton are more difficult to secure than wool because there is no fuzz to incorporate into the following stitches. When finishing a strand of thread, weave it in and out of the wrong side of the canvas as you would wool; only here again, take more precautions and give it a few more thrusts through other threads to make it secure.

Phulkari

BOOKENDS

JIFFY TOTE BAG

Jiffy Tote Bag

Tip of Leaf, Leaf, Diagonal Leaf, Tent, Milanese, Horizontal Milanese Stitches

This is a speedy project measured by the standards of a needlepoint timetable. A tote bag in the shape of a cylinder, it measures 24 inches in circumference and 10 inches in height. The painted fish design that constitutes the front half of the bag was purchased as a pillow. The back of the bag was worked on a plain piece of canvas of the same size. The front and the back were joined together by two seams on either side. The bag was worked on #12 canvas threads to the inch with 2-ply Persian yarn throughout. The background and the design each took about ten hours to complete.

The fish would be a pretty stunning specimen in any sea. The shapes and colors of its scales make an alluring prospect for the use of brilliant colors and ornamental stitches, particularly the leaf-shaped stitches. These leaflike stitch units are meaningful shapes in their own right, can be used singly or in a series as a border and background, and are always interesting to do. Wherever an oval or teardrop shape is required, we have the choice of the Leaf, the Fern, or the Cretan stitches. Each has the accommodating feature of being made larger, smaller, fatter, or thinner by adding to or subtracting from the length or width of the stitches that make up the sides of the shape, so they are stitches well suited to many designs. I used the **Tip of Leaf** stitch for the top of the scales and the **Leaf** for the remainder of my fish. When the oval shape pointed in an angular direction, I used the **Diagonal Leaf.** This treatment of the scales made the fish an elaborate enough catch without adding further lures, so the rest of him is done in the conservative smoothness of the **Tent** stitch. Its flatness made the scales more prominent by contrast.

Choosing colors was like going on an underwater marine expedition—blues and greens highlighted by the oranges of the reflected sun. I was mesmerized by their brilliance and needed to steady myself with the neutral shades of beige and brown for a little touch of earth.

A fish is a pretty active subject and not

Tip of Leaf, Leaf, Diagonal Leaf

particularly at home on a static background, so trying to keep him afloat with some wavelike stitches seemed a good idea. There are several wavy stitches that would qualify: the Fishbone, the Oriental, or the **Milanese.** They all make a series of triangular stitch units that have an undulating quality. I chose the Milanese stitch. For a quick durable background stitch, it is top-notch as it speeds along with the ease of a flotilla of ducks. It is durable, attractive, rhythmical to work, and it covers the canvas well. Worked in two colors, varying with each unit, the Milanese forms an elaborate stitch pattern. In one color, it makes a pleasing triangular background design. Usually it is a series of stitch units, each with four stitches graduated in length, worked diagonally to make a series of adjoining triangles. However, in this project, I used a variation I call **Horizontal Milanese**. By working the stitches horizontally, with the triangle peak at the top, and by alternating two shades of aqua blue, the stitch made a more wavelike effect, and

suddenly the whole project had a theme. What started out like a row of cute little triangular Christmas trees suddenly emerged as waves similar to those in the background of the wall painting in the "Punt Scene" at the temple of Queen Hatshepsut in Egypt. And what had once looked like a stuffed fish in a natural history museum became the subject of an Egyptian wall painting. Maybe I should have made the sea red!

TIP OF LEAF and LEAF

Pick an area for the top center of the leaf. Make a top center stitch vertically, covering 4 horizontal threads. Return to the base hole and make a slanting stitch to the right going up 3 threads and over 1. Repeat this on the other side of the center stitch. Drop down a thread and make another slanting stitch up 3 threads and over 2. Repeat on the other side. The next two stitches, stitches #6 and #7, use the same center hole as stitches #4 and #5, radiating up 2 threads and over 2. A center vein may be inserted below the first stitch, covering 2 horizontal threads.

The Leaf stitch is a series of rays growing out from a center spine. This group of stitches may be carried on for a few rows, or it may be continued as a stripe down the entire length of a canvas. Pick a center. Slant a stitch 3 threads over and 3 up and return to center.

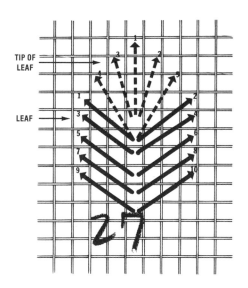

Drop down 1 thread. Repeat these slanting stitches for as long as the area requires. Match the same stitches on the opposite side of the spine, using the same center hole.

DIAGONAL LEAF

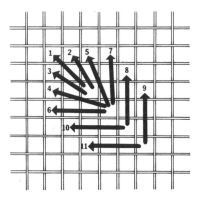

Go up 3 threads vertically, dropping down 1 stitch diagonally for each ray. The matching side will be a horizontal stitch worked over 3 threads, using the same center hole as the adjacent side.

MILANESE

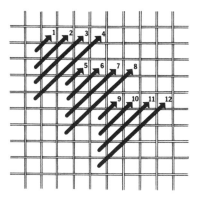

If this stitch is worked vertically or horizontally, there is no canvas distortion; if worked diagonally, slight distortion results.

Start in the upper left-hand corner and make an angle stitch (Tent stitch) over 1 in-tersection. The next stitch starts directly below and goes over 2 intersections, the third over 3, and the fourth over 4. Start with stitch 1 again and repeat the sequence. These units will follow diagonally down the canvas. The second row or the alternate row must saw-tooth into the first row and this takes a little doing. Rather than fret over the count, find the shortest stitch down near the bottom row and put a 4 intersection stitch next to it and from there build your triangle or decrease it as the case may be.

Left-handed workers should start in the lower right-hand corner.

HORIZONTAL MILANESE

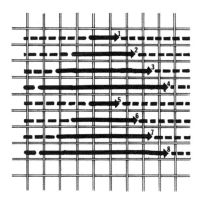

This variation is worked horizontally on the same principle as the regular Milanese. Make a half square with the first stitch stretching horizontally, covering 8 canvas threads. Directly below, decrease 1 stitch at each end, making a stitch covering 6 threads, then 4, and then 2. This is a speedy method. Skip 8 threads and do another unit, repeating these units across the canvas. Change thread color and fill in the vacant areas with stitches over 2 threads, then 4, 6, and 8.

Bookends

Shadow Box, Stacked Cube Stitches

To find unusual bookends is often difficult, but making them with a covering of needlepoint is a simple task with an attractive result. With a block or two of wood (the one illustrated is a 4-inch cube) and a canvas pattern in the shape of a cross, the project is well on its way. Almost any stitch pattern or design is suitable. The center section or top of the cube, I did in the **Shadow Box** stitch pattern and the sides in the **Stacked Cube** stitch pattern. Both were worked on a blank piece of #18 canvas threads to the inch. I used French silk in full ply, which covers well. If embroidery cotton is used, it should also be in full ply; for Persian yarn, 2 ply is recommended.

The Shadow Box is perfect for those who like to work with many different changes in color. Subtle shading in at least three colors is the only way to effect the shadow. Although five would be ideal, I used four in this case. The shading goes from dark on the left side to light on the right.

The Stacked Cube on the sides of the

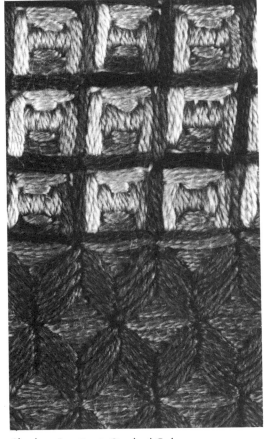

Shadow Box (top), *Stacked Cube*

See color picture opposite page 80   **85**

block pattern can be done in two very closely related shades of silk. However, in this instance, although only one color is used for both sides, the light reflections make it appear as if there were two. With wool two colors are definitely needed. The top of the unit is done in a lighter shade of the same color.

These two stitch patterns give the needleworker a marvelous opportunity to experiment with color values. Both are recommended only for small squared areas. It would be fairly impossible to use them where any compensating stitch is required to round out or finish up an area.

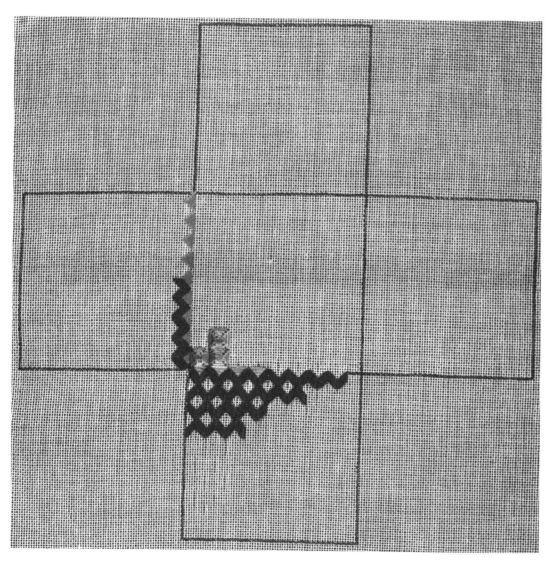

SHADOW BOX

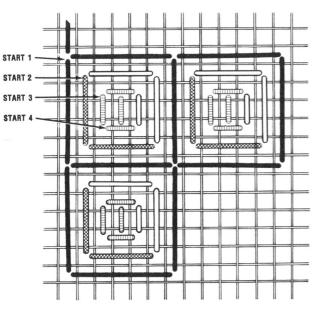

START 1
START 2
START 3
START 4

The Shadow Box is a series of horizontal and vertical stitches forming a square unit. The outside edge of the square box covers 6 threads, and these outside stitches share holes with the neighboring boxes whenever possible. The next, or inner, layer of stitches covers 4 threads forming a smaller box, and the inside center forms a shutter area with 3 vertical stitches covering 2 threads and 2 horizontal stitches, also covering 2 threads, edging the top and bottom of the shutter. Because of the thread change, it does become a bit tedious, but otherwise, it is a simple and trim pattern. Its squared units make an attractive border, particularly effective in a modern piece.

STACKED CUBE

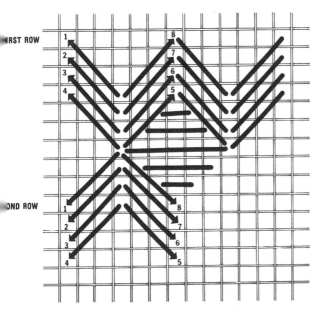

FIRST ROW

SECOND ROW

The Stacked Cube is a stitch pattern similar to the Leaf stitch except that the cubes are restricted to 4 stitches forming the sides of a box. Make vertical rows of 4 stitches slanting over 3 vertical and horizontal threads. The lower end of the 4 stitches forms a center path. From this center path, make another 4 stitches ascending 3 vertical and horizontal stitches. This makes the second side of the cube. Continue these two-sided cubes across or down the canvas to cover the area desired. The second row will start with descending slanting stitches directly below or next to these units, also covering the same number of threads. The top of the cube is filled with 5 horizontal stitches covering 2 threads, 4, 6, 4, 2. This will fill in the area in the form of a tilted square. It is difficult to determine just where the first small stitch for the cube top should start, but by parting the threads slightly, you can see the area that will accommodate the small horizontal stitch covering 2 threads.

Telephone-Book Cover

Split Encroached Gobelin, Slanted Encroached Gobelin, Upright Encroached Gobelin, Plaited Gobelin, Mosaic, Crossed Mosaic, Tent Stitches

An array of angular shapes makes up this fairly abstract design of orchids, which in this project was used as a cover for a telephone book. It is worked on #10 canvas threads to the inch with 3-ply Persian yarn in some stitches and 2-ply in others. This change in the thickness of the yarn is necessary because otherwise some of the stitches chosen will not cover the canvas adequately and others will be too bulky. I have used seven ornamental stitches as well as the **Tent** stitch in this design.

The designer seemed to be as interested in the shapes surrounding the abstract orchids as in the flowers themselves, so this is a great opportunity for the needlepointer to make the background shapes as dominant as the main subject. I chose four Gobelin stitches (there are many more variations) for this piece, not only for their appropriateness for my interpretation of the design, but also because they are durable stitches. Few things get more use in the average household than the telephone book, un-

less it is the telephone, so practical, non-snagging stitches are a requirement. Many Gobelin stitches encroach, or overlap, which makes them sturdy without being coarse. They are, in fact, the smoothest and softest of all the canvas-embroidery stitches. The encroaching makes them excellent for shading because when the stitches are worked in close shades, they flow together like wax colors in a candle.

Choosing colors for an abstract may appear to be a simple matter, for there is no need to stick to a realistic color scheme. But as in all design, each shape must have a meaning. This is usually done by making the abstract forms and colors relate to other shapes and colors in the design. It would be easy to go all out and select a rainbow of personal favorites, but unless some rules are followed, the design may end up looking like the tag end of a canapé tray. I found this to be true in my own selection of colors for this project, and after I had assembled what I wanted for shading, I re-

88   See color picture opposite page 65

membered the phrase, "Something light, something bright, something dark, and something neutral," and discarded some of the more vivid colors.

Orchids are as smooth as velvet and very delicately shaded. Even though this was an abstract design, I wanted to represent the flowers with a smooth textured stitch and in mild, neutral colors. I decided on the **Split Encroached Gobelin** stitch worked horizontally and vertically and two shades of beige for the petals, and the **Slanted Encroached Gobelin** and a slightly darker beige for the trumpet. The combination of a muted color

scheme with soft stitches keeps them in low key. Only for the neck of the orchid did I get away from the neutral treatment by choosing the **Upright Encroached Gobelin** and a brilliant coral color. The small orchids in jagged star shapes resembled dancing figures, and though they, too, should be kept muted, they did not have to convey the smooth elegance of the larger orchids. Angular shapes could take an angular stitch, so I chose the **Plaited Gobelin,** the coarsest of all the Gobelin stitches. It is a series of stitch units worked in opposing alternating angles. For the color, I picked a soft light green.

The shapes around the flowers seemed to be dark shadow areas, so I decided upon a dark shade of green, which would make them important and bring out the background, and a heavy patterned stitch, the **Mosaic.** It is a coarse repetitive unit of 3 stitches, and its neat firm texture contrasts well with the softness of the Gobelin stitches. The centers of the flowers were good areas in which to use some lumpy stitch units. The **Crossed Mosaic,** which has a slightly more elevated but less embossed look than the plain Mosaic, seemed a good choice. At this point I knew from experience it was wise to consider the number of stitches chosen, and use some caution in selecting a stitch for the remaining area, which might be thought of as the sky. A conservative choice would, of course, be the **Tent** stitch. With all the other earthy tans and greens, a nice sky blue made a delightful color contrast.

The Gobelin stitches are not straight from the Gobelin tapestry factory in France, as one might assume, but originated in the Orient millennia ago. They

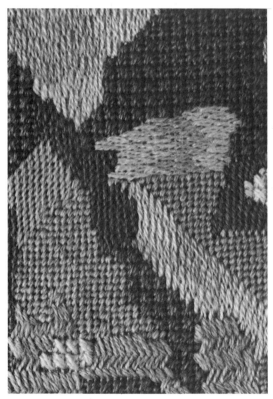

From top left down, *Split Encroached Gobelin, Upright Encroached Gobelin, Slanted Encroached Gobelin, Tent, Plaited, Crossed Mosaic,* Upper right, *Mosaic*

have been called Gobelin stitches in the modern age of embroidery because they closely resemble tapestry weaving. Quite a few examples of needlework using these Gobelin tapestry weave stitches have survived the rigors of five hundred years and can be seen in museums today. Their smoothness belies their durability. They sound like the ideal stitch for any situation, and they are, if they are encroaching. If they are not, like all upright stitches, they need a careful correlation between the heaviness of the yarn and the size of the canvas mesh. If this cannot be accomplished, painting the surface of the canvas is advised.

MOSAIC

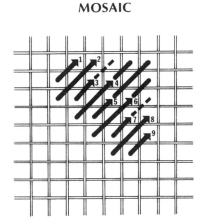

Start from upper left, make a Tent stitch angling over 1 intersection. Drop down 1 stitch and make an angle stitch up 2 vertical and 2 horizontal rows. To the right of the bottom of the last stitch, make another Tent stitch. This will make a small square. The stitch unit consists of 3 stitches: 1 short, 1 long, and 1 short, each unit sharing the last short stitch. These units may be worked across the canvas horizontally, up or down vertically, or on a diagonal. When worked in a diagonal line, a rhythm is easy to pick up, but there will be a slight stretching of the canvas to one side.

Left-handed workers should start at the bottom right and work up and across to the left. Here, too, the units may be worked across the canvas horizontally, up or down vertically, or across the canvas diagonally.

CROSSED MOSAIC

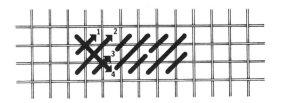

Make a square box as in the regular Mosaic, but add a diagonal stitch that will cross the entire square of the stitch unit.

SPLIT ENCROACHED GOBELIN

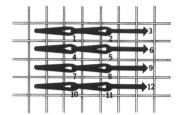

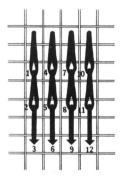

SLANTED ENCROACHED GOBELIN

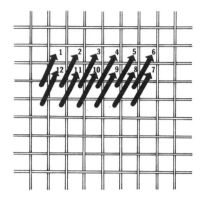

This is also a very attractive, neat stitch and requires no painted surface. The slanted stitches make it more subtle as a shading stitch than the Upright Encroached Gobelin. There will be a very slight degree of distortion to the canvas, but keeping the threads loose seemed to help me with this problem.

Start from left to right. Make a row of slightly slanted stitches going over 2 horizontal threads and over 1 vertical thread. Drop down 1 horizontal thread from the first stitch of the first row. Again go over 2 horizontal threads and over 1 vertical thread. The top of the stitch will overlap the bottom of the stitch of the preceding row.

UPRIGHT ENCROACHED GOBELIN

This is a true marching stitch, precise, erect, neat, and causing no canvas distortion. It would be beautiful worked in Bargello patterns, and the overlapping would eliminate the gap between rows. It makes an interwoven effect that is effective in delicate shading. Because of the encroaching stitch, a 3-ply yarn on the #10 and #12 canvas threads to

This is a most satisfying stitch, perfect for large areas as well as small. In the illustration, it is shown worked in the horizontal as well as the vertical. It gives a nice long sweep to a design and perhaps most closely resembles the Gobelin tapestry stitch. It is also superb for fine shading.

It can be started horizontally or vertically from the top right or left, and is worked in the same way as the previous stitches but instead of putting the encroaching stitch to the side as in the Upright or Diagonal Gobelins, the encroaching stitch actually splits the bottom of the thread of the stitch in the previous row. The rows become enmeshed, and a lovely smooth texture results. The stitch can cover from 2 to 6 threads.

Left-handed workers will find it easier to start at top left.

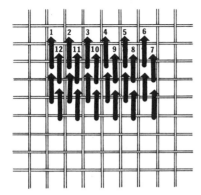

the inch will cover the canvas, but with a 2-ply yarn, unless you want to bother with a painted surface on the canvas, you should use a smaller #14 size canvas.

For the Vertical Encroached Gobelin, start from left to right. Work a vertical stitch covering 2 or more horizontal threads of canvas. In the next row, the stitches overlap the preceding row by 1 thread. The overlapping stitch may be inserted to either the right or the left of the stitch in the previous row, but once a side has been selected, all succeeding stitches must rest on that side.

To make the Horizontal Encroached Gobelin, a horizontal stitch covering 2 or more vertical rows of the canvas would be covered. It can be worked from either the top or the bottom.

Work from left to right horizontally, or from top left, work down vertically. If working from left to right horizontally, make a slanting stitch *down* over 4 vertical and 2 horizontal threads. For the next stitch go to the left under 1 vertical thread and make a slanting stitch *up* over 4 vertical and 2 horizontal threads. Repeat these alternating slanting stitches across the row.

Left-handed workers should start from right to left.

If starting from the top left, when working down vertically, make a series of vertical stitches slanting *down* over 4 vertical and 2 horizontal threads, skipping every other hole. The second row is worked from the bottom *up*, starting 1 thread to the left of bottom of last stitch. This will overlap and cross the first vertical row. Next row will start from top again.

Left-handed workers should start from lower right.

Byzantine Eyeglass Case

Star, Bargello, Knitting, Hungarian, Byzantine Stitches

Geometric patterns are popular among needlepointers. Perhaps the reason is the lack of regimentation required in comparison to the concern one feels when trying to re-create a representational object. Creating or working on a geometric design with a theme in mind, I find the most rewarding.

I had always wanted a dressy eyeglass case, one that could be whipped out with a flair and that felt good to the touch. I decided that a design done in silk with a Byzantine look would be lovely. Domes, spires, and curves, the main features of Byzantine architecture, are repeated in Byzantine designs and decorations as well.

Since I wanted to use silk, I had an unlimited array of colors from which to select. French silk has a dye chart with so many colors that picking from it is like choosing a favorite butterfly. On #14 canvas threads to the inch, full-ply French silk covers the canvas well for long upright stitches, those mostly used

in this project. French silk is very similar to Persian yarn in the amount used to cover an inch. I chose two blues, two aquas, two purples, and two reds—a stunning combination.

I made a diamond shape out of that tiny stitch the **Star** by making three stitch units across the center, then adding two more above, and then one unit for the top, worked in alternating shades of blue. By adding an eardrop on the lower sides of the diamond, I hoped a Byzantine onion shape might develop. It didn't, but a charming little pattern appeared that was so appealing and the Star stitch is such fun to do, so I made two rows of them evenly spaced.

The Star, also called Eyelet, and Piesteek in Scotland, is often used in clumps for texturized and lacelike designs. During the Victorian era, men's carpet slippers were often decorated with it. It seems a dainty stitch for such a purpose, but then those stern-looking Victorian males would put up with most anything to keep

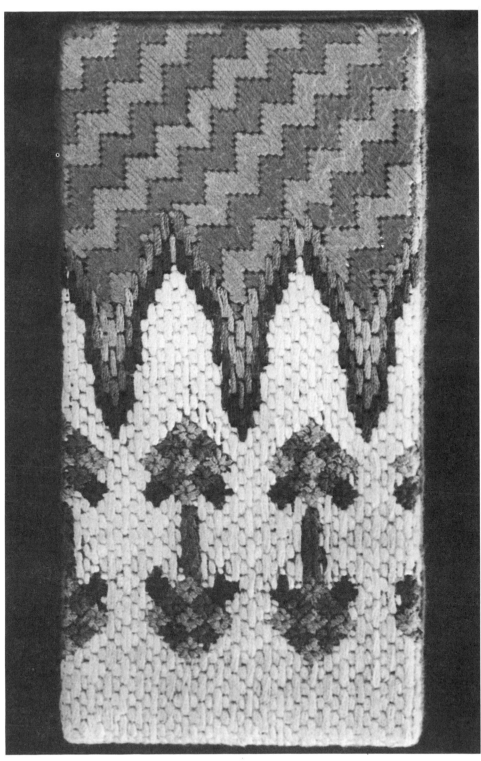

the ladies busy and away from their port and cigars. Today in northern Portugal, one sees it worked into the fabulous skirts of the women of the Minho River area.

The **Bargello** makes lovely spires and arches (see page 64), so I worked niches of this stitch in two shades of purple around the Star stitch design. The Bargello is most frequently associated with large allover patterns for chairs, pillows, and benches. It is too often forgotten as a charming addition to a needlepoint composition where it can often be used effectively in small areas. As a border, its subtle color graduations can be helpful in funneling the eye toward a center design. It is successful as a accent where a smooth texture is required. It can also be used with distinction as a pattern on the four mitered sides of a pillow when the face of the pillow is done in another stitch.

To connect these floating rows, I chose the **Knitting** stitch in deep blue. It looks like stockinette stitch in knitting, and it is very similar to the Chain stitch, too, but it is not worked in loops. As a sturdy straight stem stitch, it is superb, and it is also excellent when used as a heavy outline stitch for vertical or horizontal runs, or as an occasional stripe in a background pattern.

The background for these rows is in the **Hungarian** stitch in two shades of aqua. This upright stitch, which makes a series of diamond shapes, is similar in execution to Bargello, but is uses shorter stitches and is more restrained, confining itself to a small delightful pattern. Its smooth satin look makes a very dignified effect, and it is in exquisite taste no matter where or on what it is used. Particularly attractive done in alternating colors, it moves along rapidly, and with the proper balance between weight of yarn and size mesh of canvas, it covers the canvas extremely well for an upright stitch. Although mostly used for background work or borders, it could go well in any small angular area. For a whimsical effect, try using it to decorate a spotted animal, using alternating colors for each unit. Because of its small stitches, it adapts nicely to small objects like purses, belts, and pincushions.

TIGER-CAT PILLOW

CHINESE-BUTTERFLY PILLOW

The Hungarian stitch was brought to Europe by those needle-happy Moors and put into the hands of Queen Gisela, a sister of the German emperor Henry II, in the eleventh century. A great needlewoman, she set up an embroidery workshop near her palace in Hungary for production as well as teaching. From there, the stitch became popular throughout Europe and was called *Point de Hongrie*.

The other part of the background, I worked in the **Byzantine** in two shades of red. This stitch reflects the regularity of design that was part of the new art form developed with the founding of the Byzantine Empire. It is a structural stitch, geometric in concept. Needleworkers like doing it and are usually pleased with the results. When worked in two shades of one color, it has the subtlety of velvet, and like velvet, when the light changes, so does the color. Worked in silk thread, it has a luster and sheen that rivals a lovely damask. Because of its patterned regularity, it is an ideal background stitch, but like many other geometric stitches, it shows up at its best in a small area against a variant. In a design where a flat surface is required, this offshoot of the Satin stitch works well, and its simple elegance makes a handsome border. Each stitch is worked on a slant, and like the light and shadow falling on temple steps, sections of stitches form patterns of steps.

The upright stitches, the slanting stitches, and the tiny starlike motif are

From top, *Byzantine, Bargello, Hungarian, Star, Knitting*

lovely together, and though I had hoped my geometric design would turn out a wholly Byzantine motif, it looked more like a Persian garden—at least it was in the same part of the world. A finished geometric design, unless sketched beforehand, rarely resembles the original concept. Though this sort of design exploration may seem too free to many needleworkers, it can be very gratifying.

STAR

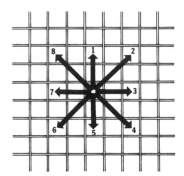

BARGELLO

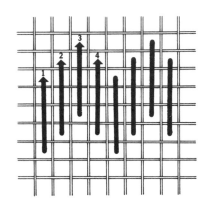

The Star is made with 8 points radiating from a center hole like the other "Eye" stitches. Each stitch covers 2 threads. The stitch units form into a square.

The Bargello used in this project covers 4 horizontal stitches making an upright series of stitches in the form of arches. For directions, see Bargello pillow on page 64.

HUNGARIAN

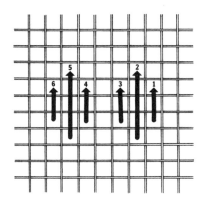

BYZANTINE

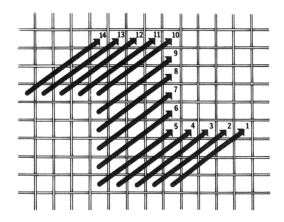

Each unit forms a small hexagon with the first stitch going upright over 2 horizontal threads, the second over 4, and the third over 2. *Omit* a stitch and then repeat the 2, 4, 2 pattern again. In the second row the short stitches always come underneath the short stitches and the long under the long of the previous row, so you have a vertical row of shorts and a vertical row of longs. Repeat the same count filling in the empty space with a long stitch.

In a horizontal row, make 5 slanting stitches going over 4 vertical threads and up 3 horizontal threads to make each stitch. Change direction and, going up, make 5 horizontal stitches slanting in the same manner. The corner stitches (#5 and #10) are counted twice.

KNITTING

This stitch climbs from bottom to top and then reverses and descends from top to bottom. Make a slanting stitch up 4 horizontal threads and over 1 vertical thread to the right. Come out 2 horizontal threads down and 1 vertical thread to the left. Repeat this to top. At top, come out 2 threads to the left and slant 4 horizontal threads down and 1 vertical thread to the left. Come out 2 horizontal threads up and 1 vertical thread to the left, and slant down 4 horizontal threads and 1 vertical thread to the right, and continue down to end of row.

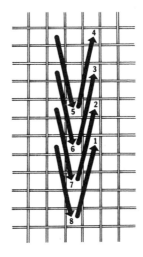

Tiger-Cat Pillow

Turkey Knot, Tent Stitches

A whimsical touch, a bit of fluff, can make an animal irresistible. A lion's mane, a poodle's topknot, or anything that calls for a fuzzy accent is perfect for the **Turkey Knot** stitch. This very bold tiger cat, for instance, becomes less menacing when softened with a woolly patch of fur on his paws and tail. The pillow illustrated is worked in **Tent** stitch on #10 canvas threads to the inch with 3-ply Persian yarn. The only novelty stitch in this project is the Turkey Knot, and the yarn used is the same weight as that of the background.

The Turkey Knot is a very clever stitch. It can make a tufting, fringe, or shag effect with little effort. It is made with a series of loops locked so securely by a back stitch that it can be used for rugs or similar utilitarian articles, small or large. It is the most bulky of the textured stitches and a voracious yarn-eater. When used as a grounding, covering an entire surface, there is no necessity to consider texture relationships, but when combined with other stitch patterns in a de-

sign, its use and extent of use must be considered with care. Too much texture may lead to disaster.

The Turkey Knot stitch may be used in three ways. The first way, an uncut succession of loops, makes a handsome fringe in a Mediterranean style ideal for edging pillows, rugs, or other needle-pointed objects that may need to be softened with a trimming. Because the stitch is worked in vertical rows, there are numerous opportunities for variations in yarn colors. It is easy to alternate the color combinations or to graduate the colors by changing yarn each row. When the colors are shaded, the result is a fringe resembling the trim used on curtains and portiers from the Victorian past. This versatility of color usage opens up many decorating possibilities.

The second way is the shag effect, that look so popular in Scandinavia and now a hit in America. It is preferable to use a heavy yarn for this. Whether the loops are cut or uncut, they will make a rough, nappy texture. The size of the loops is a

personal preference, but a thumb's worth is a good gauge. Simple geometric designs entirely in Turkey Knot worked in heavy yarn on a large mesh canvas can make a stunning piece.

The third way to use the stitch is as a clump of fuzz in an area of design. This is done by cutting the loops to within ¼

Turkey Knot

inch of the canvas. Here again the use of soft or heavy yarn is desirable, in order to get as thick a pile as possible. To produce a piled texture in such an easy way is so fascinating that a caution light must be flashed to limit the worker's enthusiasm. Making fluffy tufts at every available opportunity can become too coy. The Turkey Knot stitch, like garlic, must be sparingly used.

The name, Turkey Knot, might suggest the crest of an edible bird, but it actually comes from the stitch's similarity to rugs and mats of heavy pile which were imported to England from Turkey as early as the Elizabethan period and to America in the early eighteenth century. The adaptation of this tufted work for household use was known as "set work" or "Turkey Work." In early American homes the "Turkey Work" table cover and the "turkey worker" were almost as common as the spinning wheel and the spinner.

The instructions and diagrams for the heavy textured stitches often sound so complicated that they may send one into shock, but in this case, fringe- and fluff-making is really only a simple back stitch with the alternating stitch extended, so that it forms a loop and the taut stitch forms a lock around the loop.

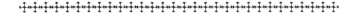

TURKEY KNOT

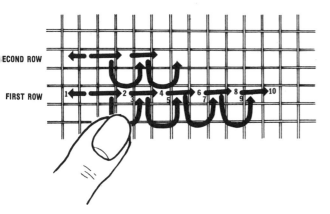

SECOND ROW

FIRST ROW

All the earlier stitches we have discussed have started with the needle coming from the back of the canvas through to the front. Here is the first exception. Start in the lower left-hand corner of the area to be covered and work the stitch rows from bottom to top. From the front of the canvas, make a single horizontal stitch going *under* 1 vertical thread from right to left. This will leave an unattached tail on the surface. Hold this tail down with the left thumb and proceed with a flat back stitch. Work across the row from left to right, going forward to the right over 2 threads and back to the left *under* 1 thread. Repeat going to the right and the left over 1, but this time form a loop (hold with the left thumb) splitting the yarn of the previous stitch when making this loop stitch, thereby locking it. Alternate the flat back stitch and the loop back stitch across the row. In this piggy-back manner, each stitch will overlap 1 thread. At the end of the row, secure the thread, cut it, and start the second row again at the left side 2 threads up, and stagger the rotation of the loop and lock stitches from the preceding row. Varying the lengths of the loops makes interesting texture patterns, but a uniform size makes a neater trim. If tufting is the objective, however, there is no need to worry about the loops being the same size because they will be cut and then cropped to a "butch" haircut of 1/4 inch.

Left-handed workers should start at bottom right and work to the left and up.

Chinese-Butterfly Pillow

Rococo, Algerian Eye, Double Straight Cross, Tent, Cretan, Ray Stitches

Ancient Chinese design has a unique beauty that cannot be surpassed. Perhaps the secret lies in its simplicity and serenity. During the great twelfth-century flowering of the arts, many new surface and canvas-embroidery stitches were devised for all types of needlework, and examples of this handwork were carried to the Western world. Many of our present stitches resemble the early Chinese stitches but are done on a very much larger scale, for the Chinese work was so fine that even if we had eyes like birds, we could not hope to simulate it. One stitch was even named the "Forbidden Stitch" by the emperor after so many of his subjects went blind while working it. Although any copy of an original Chinese work of art may lack a certain reverence and mystery, by using Chinese colors and palette and by choosing appropriate textures, the needlepointer can reproduce an exquisite creation done in the Oriental manner.

The butterfly in this pillow is closely associated with early Chinese symbolism and is seen on designs of the twelfth century. Flight and movement were often a part of Chinese design motifs. Even Chinese garments suggested wings and ease of movement. By a careful selection of stitch and color, it is possible to capture a bit of that spirit as well as stimulate the exquisite luminous quality of the butterfly's wings. The design was worked on #14 canvas threads to the inch, using French silk in its full ply of 7 strands for the design and 2-ply Persian yarn for the background.

In search of an exotic stitch worthy of a beautiful butterfly, the **Rococo** stitch, which historians say is very old and originated in China, became the ideal choice. It is a very charming, elaborate-looking stitch, and each stitch unit resembles a small Chinese lantern. What could be more appropriate? Each unit interlocks closely with the adjoining unit and therefore can be shaded well. The stitch has had three names in the modern world of embroidery: the Bundle stitch, which describes its mechanics but not its beauty;

the Tied stitch, a far too homely name for such a handsome stitch; and its present name Rococo, which is also inappropriate as one associates the Rococo period with swooping curves and general flamboyance. In the seventeenth century the stitch was very popular for the decoration of caskets, which are not funereal as one might suspect, but rather elaborate jewel boxes. Examples seen today in museums are in splendid condition, so the durability of the Rococo must be excellent.

The round petals of the flowers are perfect for the "Eye" stitches, which can be worked either in small units spaced in clumps or around the edge of a design. They are also delicate in appearance. The **Algerian Eye** (described on page 122) was chosen because its size and shape fit the shapes of the particular flowers in the design. The center of the flowers should be lacy too. A group of the Smyrna Cross or the **Double Straight Cross** stitches are always satisfactory for good texture and elegance. I chose the Double Straight Cross here because I think it is more exotic and builds up into a beautiful small snowflake. A cluster worked in a circle requires some filler stitches, and the **Tent**

From left, *Ray* (border), *Cretan* (leaves), *Algerian Eye* (flower),
Double Straight Cross (flower center), *Rococo* (wings)

stitch was used for this purpose. Of the many leaf-shaped stitches in our bag, the **Cretan** stitch was chosen because it is less flat, and for this design, I wanted a stitch with as much daintiness as possible. It creates a feather-like effect with each stitch unit. Its stitches lie neatly side by side, and its center anchor forms a lovely spinal column that blends well with the tied sections of the Rococo stitch. The Cretan stitch originated in the Greek islands around the tenth century.

The natives of the island of Crete used it in brilliant colors to decorate their costumes for holiday festivals. In France it is called the Persian stitch. The **Ray** stitch, or Fan stitch as it is frequently known, which fans out in an Oriental manner and works up neatly as a border stitch with no filler stitches necessary, was selected as a frame, and the Tent stitch was used in all other areas as well as for the background.

Color selection for this piece started

with the background, and as Chinese blue seems to complement any color put with it, it was the appropriate choice. The yarn market is flooded with shades of blue, but none were close to Chinese blue in hue. All seemed too vibrant or too gray. Combining two existing colors by using one strand of each was the only solution. A deep Prussian blue combined with a girl-scout green, both of the same intensity, came close to the color used in ancient Chinese porcelains. With this new color and a selection of three shades of green-gold, the yarn palette started to take on an Oriental look. A touch of apricot for the fruits and flowers, and two shades of red and coral for the butterfly made the design sing out against the blue background.

These are exciting colors, but there is such a thing as being carried away by the rainbow at one's fingertips, and that happened to me. While working along, I realized that the figures in the design seemed to be flying off into space like a display of fireworks. There was no unity, and the objects became isolated splotches like postage stamps on a package. Rather than give up my color choice, I thought that a border might discourage the Parcel Post look and restrict the design within the pillow boundaries. A border, like a picture frame, can enhance a design, but it can also, like an unsuitable frame, detract from the subject. In this case the border was successful and a delightful addition. Sometimes mistakes may lead to enrichment.

ROCOCO

A swift glance at the diagram for this stitch would send many people scurrying on to something that looks less complicated, but upon further scrutiny, it is apparent that it is merely a "bundle" of 7 stitches, 6 canvas threads long, that are spread out in a fan shape and tied together in the center with a single stitch. It is easily executed, can be worked diagonally as well as vertically, and is used very satisfactorily in small clusters. It can be shaded subtly—half of one unit in one shade and the other half in another; it can be used as a background stitch, although it would be rather slow-going if the background was of any sizable dimension. It also makes a lovely lacelike border. Compensating stitches

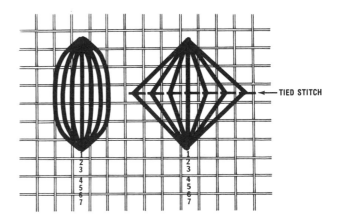

TIED STITCH

can be an angle stitch, such as a portion of the Algerian Eye, or the Tent stitch. Start at upper left of canvas, working across.

DOUBLE STRAIGHT CROSS

The reverse of the Smyrna Cross, this is simply a diagonal cross placed on top of an upright one. In this project the upright cross covers 4 canvas threads, and the diagonal cross covers 2. Each unit should be completed before going on to the next. All crosses should overlap in the same direction (see page 42).

RAY

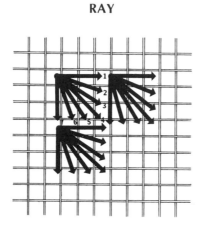

The Ray stitch is gaining in popularity as a border stitch and should be used more frequently. It can be pointed in any direction, which makes it invaluable for turning corners on a border. It is also easy to do. The direction of the rays may be alternated with each unit, or they may point only one way. Its use as a background stitch is rare, although it should be successful as a checkered effect. It is also called the Fan stitch.

Ray stitches all radiate from one corner hole to make a square. There are 7 stitches in each unit. Start the unit by making a horizontal stitch from left to right, going over 3 canvas threads. Come back to the center hole and make another stitch extending to the same parallel as the tip of the first stitch but 1 thread down. Continue this for 4 stitches, ending the vertical line, and then round the corner by making a line of 3 stitches reaching to the same parallel as #4 stitch, making a

horizontal line. This will complete the square. Continue these units in the direction indicated by the design.

CRETAN

VERTICAL

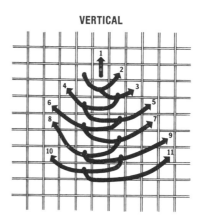

HORIZONTAL

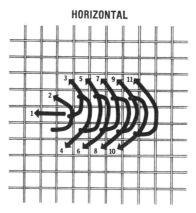

DIAGONAL

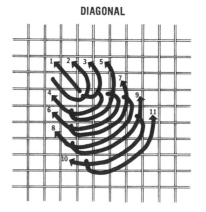

The Cretan stitch is another that unfortunately requires a complicated-looking diagram, but don't pass it by because it is really only a featherstitch swinging from side to side like a hammock. Each stitch is a loop secured in the center by the next stitch. Wherever there is an opportunity to use an oval or leaflike shape in a design, the Cretan is a worthy consideration. It can be worked vertically, horizontally, and diagonally, although the latter does not cover the canvas well and requires heavier yarn. To check on the center vein and to see that all is going well, turn the canvas to the back. If you are working the stitch on the vertical or horizontal, there should be two even tracks, railroad-tie style. If you are working the stitch on the diagonal, one side of the track will be like a Satin stitch, the other like an outline stitch.

Chinese-Patchwork Footstool

Jacquard, Diamond, Oriental, Oriental Variation, Long-Armed Cross, Tent, Fishbone, Parisian, Leviathan, Moorish Stitches

The Chinese introduced many art motifs that became fads during various periods of history. The "layered look" in embroidered mats was popular with them many years ago. By applying it to canvas embroidery, assorted ornamental stitches can be worked into paneled patterns in the manner of Chinese silk mats and hangings which are vaguely similar to American patchwork. Patchwork, however, as seen in old pillows and bedspreads is uniquely American. Frugal colonial dames hoarded bits of precious cottons, piecing them together into larger objects, and from this wholly utilitarian necessity grew a charming folk art. The Chinese, on the other hand, developed their arrangement of embroideries and silks as an art form.

This footstool design, with its isolated Chinese figures in each corner, wide center strip, and medallion in the middle, would adapt well to this patchwork treatment. By using some textured background stitches and adding borders to the design, the Chinese symbols become

a composite unit and the piece develops that layered look in the Chinese manner. It is worked on #14 canvas threads to the inch, using 2-ply Persian yarn and full-ply (7-strand) French silk.

Looking for border stitches was the first task. Not all of them are labeled as such, and it is often only through experimenting with the stitch for an inch or two on the canvas that one can see its potential. In a way, stitch units are often easier to work when used as borders rather than as background or design fillers because they do not have to sashay around curves and in and out of peninsulas the way they do when embracing a figure. On the other hand, a border must frame a design with precise measurements on all four sides. The **Jacquard** was selected as one border stitch because it is a stitch pattern of great dignity. It is also a delight to do. Perhaps its similarity to the ever-popular Greek-key pattern border or its crisp neatness makes it a favorite. It can be used subtly in closely related muted shades of one color or

boldly in opposing colors. The Jacquard is a series of steps with alternating regular Tent and elongated Tent stitches climbing up from one plateau to another. It is very similar to the Byzantine except that it has a narrow set of stairs in between a wider set of stairs. Monsieur Jacquard, a French weaver, developed a textile loom in 1803 which worked automatically on a punch-card system, something unique in those days, and with these computer cards with perforations like Pianola rolls, endless different figured materials could be woven without resetting the loom. A whole new world of patterned fabrics resulted, and the name Jacquard was heard as often in the early 1800's as the name Singer was in the

CHINESE-PATCHWORK FOOTSTOOL 111

early 1900's. The modern name for this stitch may have come from its similarity to a Jacquard design. In this design, as a border around the square with the Chinese emblem, it seemed to continue the cubed formality of that motif. It was worked in a combination of dark blue and light blue.

The **Diamond** stitch looked right for another border stitch, but when worked for a few inches, it looked too heavy for the frame of the delicate Chinese temple. By reducing the size of the diamonds, and using two colors, a charming series of diamonds and crosses appeared, perfect as a sizable border width. In two related shades it would be lovely as a background stitch, also. The Diamond stitch when worked in its full dimensions can be used with a variety of colors, and it is in itself a design that would be complete as a grounding. A series of horizontal stitches, it makes a diaper pattern with alternating rows of vertical and horizontal straight stitches as fillers. Once the diaper pattern is counted for one section, the repetitive grounding goes like the wind.

The **Oriental** stitch is similar to the

Diamond (left), *Moorish* (bottom)

Milanese and the Cashmere stitches in that it makes a series of equilateral triangle units on a diagonal with alternating rows of the units pointing in the opposite direction. The area between these alternating rows is filled with three elongated Tent stitches. This is a good pattern and background stitch and is at its best when used with contrasting colors. The **Oriental Variation** that gives a far more elaborate pattern is used here in the center strip. With two closely related shades of red, it makes a very rich-looking piece of canvas embroidery. It would work up easier as a background patterned stitch than in this narrow strip, as the triangles would not be interrupted by compensating stitches at the all too frequent appearance of the boundary. In this small area, however, working it was not too difficult, and it makes a very elaborate and handsome ribbon. The braidlike narrow border stitch that runs along the side of the center ribbon and between the squares is the old, delightfully compact, and beautiful **Long-Armed Cross** stitch used in the Handbag project on page 62. Whenever a braid effect is desired, this stitch is a beauty.

To free the design from that overly

Long-Armed Cross (edging), *Oriental Variation* (left), *Jacquard* (upper right)

CHINESE-PATCHWORK FOOTSTOOL

JACOBEAN PILLOW

framed, fussy look, two of the squares were done in textured background stitches and deliberately left without borders. The background stitch of the bordered squares is the **Tent** stitch. In the fish square, the **Fishbone** stitch was selected, not because it bore the name of the subject but because when used in two shades of blue, it looked a little like waves. The Fishbone stitch is heavy when not used as a braid or border. It is made with a sharply slanted stitch having a cross-stitch at one end, which forms a trim edge. It is similar to the Herringbone with one angle stitch very long.

The **Parisian** stitch was chosen for the background of the bat corner because its upright stitches act as a relief from all the other angle stitches. It is a series of long and short stitches with the short stitch always under the long stitch of the preceding row. This is helpful to know when starting a new row. It is an almost identical unit to work as the Hungarian, except that in the Hungarian each *long* stitch is under the long stitch of the preceding row. The Parisian works up quickly and can cover a large area effectively. If using a dark color, a painted canvas surface of the same color or one of the same intensity is suggested.

The center of the medallion is done in the **Leviathan,** one of the oldest of stitches. It is a spider-like cross-stitch with each angle stitch radiating from a center hole forming a square. The center stitch is an Upright Cross stitch.

The last layer and border is worked in the **Moorish** stitch. This, like the Jacquard and Scotch stitches, is banded by the Tent stitch. This series of connecting squares worked on a diagonal and bordered by the Tent makes an appealing pattern of blocks and striations. The Moors were masters at producing design out of the most elementary forms, so it is not surprising that this very simple but elegant combination of squares and zigzags suggests a Moorish design. The stitch makes a charming border if worked in a wide band and is perfect when used for a pattern design within an object. It has, moreover, two aspects. When two contrasting colors are used, it boldly zigzags down the canvas like the steps of a pyramid, but when worked in two close shades of the same color, it has the lovely subtlety of fine lace. Used as the outside border on this Chinese conglomerate, it adds the final touch to the "layered" cake.

The colors selected for this piece had to be exotic but in good taste, in keeping with all Chinese design. Shades of blue, red, and gold predominate. The objects in the squares were done in the Tent stitch and are worked in silk.

Fishbone (upper left), *Parisian* (lower right), *Leviathan* (center star)

ORIENTAL   ORIENTAL VARIATION

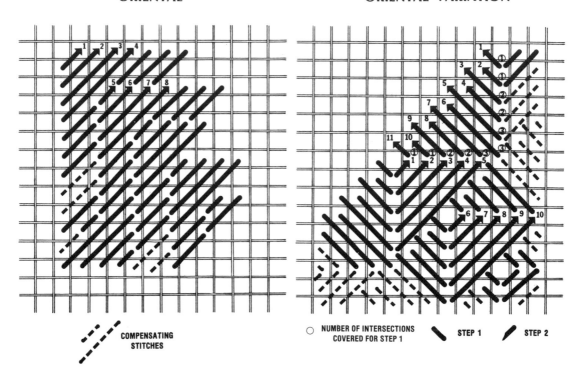

COMPENSATING STITCHES

○ NUMBER OF INTERSECTIONS COVERED FOR STEP 1   ＼ STEP 1   ／ STEP 2

Start in upper left-hand corner. Make a diagonally worked triangle, starting the first stitch covering 1 intersection, the second stitch over 2 intersections, 3 over 3, and 4 over 4. Start a second triangle with the first stitch under the center of the last triangle stitch covering 1 intersection, then over 2, 3, and 4 as in first triangle. With the second row of diagonal triangles, work them in the opposite direction with the point facing downward. The longest stitch of the first row will line up with the longest stitch of the following row. There will be a space between these diagonal units, and the filler for these spaces will be slanting stitches covering 2 intersections worked in units of 3.

Step 1: Start at upper right and make a triangle with slanting stitches going from lower left to upper right covering intersections of 1, 1, 2, 2, 3, 3 directly below each other. The bottom of these stitches will be in a vertical line. There will be 6 stitches in this angle. Now still slanting the stitches from lower right to upper left and with the bottom of each stitch on a horizontal, make stitches covering intersections of 3, 4, 4, 1, 1. There will be 5 stitches in this angle. This completes the triangle with the diagonal side zigzagging downhill. Make a series of these triangles down to the left, skipping a row between each unit.

Step 2: The area not covered will accommodate the triangles as they were made in the regular Oriental stitch with 1 more stitch added at the base. Fill in the areas, starting at the top of each vacant area, covering 1, 2, 3, 4, and 5 intersections. The triangles in this variation are not reversed as they are in the regular Oriental stitch. In other words, all small stitches of the triangles are at the top.

Note: It is very important that Step 1 be done before Step 2 as there is an overlap of stitches in Step 2.

JACQUARD

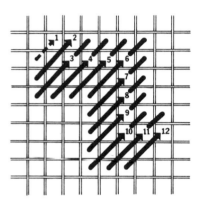

This is a series of 5 slanting stitches in zigzag segments done in the Satin and the Tent stitches. To make a border 7 rows wide, start at upper left-hand corner and make a single Tent stitch. Under this make 1 slanting stitch worked over 2 rows. (These are compensating stitches.) Now start a zigzag of 4 stitches across, slanting over 2 rows, and a unit of 4 stitches going down, and another 4-stitch unit going across. Actually the count for each segment is 5, but the center corner is counted twice, once horizontally and once vertically. The second step is to follow the zigzag pattern with a Continental stitch bordering both sides.

Left-handed workers should start at lower right of canvas. Make one compensating Tent stitch and 5 stitches across, slanting over 2 rows. Then work 4 vertical stitches, then 4 horizontal, all slanting over 2 rows. Now border this zigzag with the Tent stitch.

DIAMOND

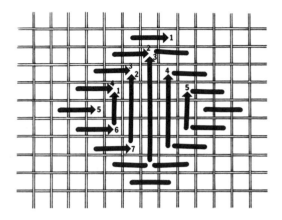

REDUCED DIAMOND

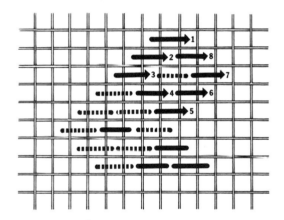

With straight horizontal stitches going over 2 threads, make a diamond with 5 stitches in each angle, moving each stitch one canvas stitch to the right or left as the angle dictates. Fill the center area with rows of vertical or horizontal stitches covering 2, 4, 6, 4, 2 canvas threads.

MOORISH

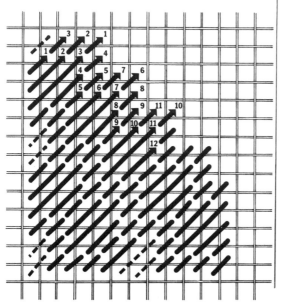

LEFT HAND

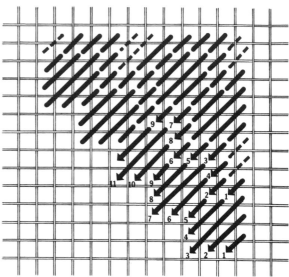

these boxes diagonally up and across the canvas. Border these connected boxes with the Tent stitch, following the numerals on the diagram.

FISHBONE

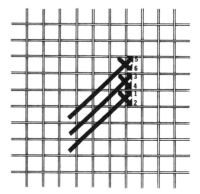

Start at the top left of the area to be covered. Drop down a thread and make a Tent stitch. Drop down 1 thread and make an angle stitch covering 2 threads up and 2 threads over. Drop down another thread and make an angle stitch 3 threads up and 3 threads over. On a horizontal line with the bottom of the last stitch, make an angle stitch 2 threads up and 2 threads over. Make a single Tent stitch with the bottom on this same horizontal line and continue these boxes across the canvas diagonally. Border these connected boxes with the Tent stitch. The count for the Tent stitch will be 3 for each riser and 3 for each step, counting the center stitch twice. When working the Tent stitch border, the stitch sequence will have to be altered. In order to avoid making a cordlike half stitch, the stitches cannot be worked consecutively. Follow numerals on diagram.

Left-handed workers should start at the lower right of area to be covered. Make a Tent stitch, then an angle stitch over 2, over 3, over 2, and then another Tent stitch; continue

Starting at lower left, make a long angle stitch going up 4 horizontal rows and over 4 vertical rows. Put a reverse Tent stitch across the top end of the stitch. For the second long stitch, start up a thread from bottom of first stitch. Repeat these stitches working vertically up the canvas. Alternate direction of rows for the wavy effect.

PARISIAN

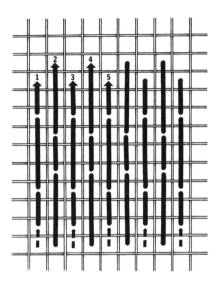

LEVIATHAN

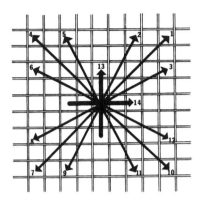

Starting at top left of work, make a vertical stitch over 2 threads, then drop down a thread and make a vertical over 4 threads, up and over 2, then 4, then 2, and repeat this across the row. In the second row the long stitches will fit under the short stitches of the preceding row.

Left-handed workers should start at bottom left.

This is a stitch very similar to the Algerian Eye with a Straight Cross stitch as the center. It is a series of 12 stitches radiating from a center hole that forms an eye.

Make a slanting stitch up 4 threads and over 4. Return to center and make the next stitch to the left up 4 and over 2, which will put the needle in 2 holes to the left of the first stitch. The third stitch is to the right of the first stitch up 2 and over 4 which will put needle in 2 threads below the second stitch. This group of 3 stitches is continued in the corners of a square. There will be an open space between each group, and this is filled with a Straight Cross covering 4 threads in the middle.

Jacobean Pillow

Algerian Eye, Spider Web, French Knot, Buttonhole, Fern, Tent Stitches

If you want to have a good time using as many stitches as you like without fear of overloading a design with too much texture, pick a pattern similar to those used in crewel work—a spray of flowers or fruit. Most frequently these are designs representing a portion of the stylized "Tree of Life" pattern, which can be traced back to the English Jacobean period in the seventeenth century and has been popular with embroiderers ever since. These patterns are a needlepointer's paradise. Delicate fruits and flowers in riotous colors branch out from a single laden stem, and the more stitches that are used, the more exciting the design becomes. So, with lots of color and an endless array of stitches, the lid is off. Always charming, these patterns can be used with almost any decor. Their primitive quality is pleasing with the austerity of early American furnishings; they complement the restfulness of contemporary Nordic designs; and they are, of course,

very much at home with English furnishings of the seventeenth and eighteenth centuries.

The design illustrated was made into a pillow, although these patterns were first commonly used for embroidery on wing chairs in England and later in America. The design would make a wonderful footstool, too, because it can be viewed from any angle and all sides look as if "this side is up." It is a 13-inch square and is done on #12 canvas threads to the inch. This size canvas lends itself to the ornamental stitches I selected because with 2-ply Persian yarn, both angle and upright stitches cover the canvas well.

In this design the flowers are the most important feature. They should dominate in both color and texture while the leaves, stems, and background should recede. With these circumstances, choosing the colors is a breeze. Any colors or color combinations for the flowers is accept-

able as long as all are about equal in value, so that one will not overpower the other. If the colors are more intense in one of the flowers it would be distracting. Dull green for the leaves and stems with neutral gold for the background keep these elements where they belong.

Selecting the stitches was the most fun, for many shapes in the design seemed to accommodate several different ones. For instance, some decorative parts of the flowers are made in circles, some smaller than others. There are several stitches in the needlepoint repertoire that make perfect rounds: the **Algerian Eye,** the **Spider Web,** and the **French Knot,** all of which I used in this project. (Another good round stitch is the Circular Couching stitch which is described in the Bicycle Seat project on page 49.)

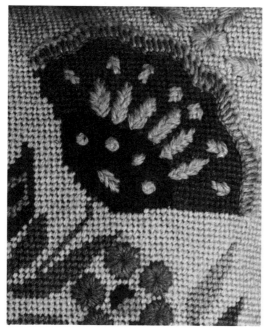

From top, *Buttonhole, Fern, French Knot, Algerian Eye*

120   JACOBEAN PILLOW

The French Knot, called French Dot in France, a nubby little buttoned-down stitch, was best for the smallest circles because it forms a single dot. This is a wonderful stitch for an accent, for the eye of an animal, or when used in a clump as a flower center. I have seen it used as the body of a lamb, and it looked for all the world like a woolly new-born lamb. The Algerian Eye was perfect for the larger rounds. One of Algeria's most decorative stitches, it is a wheel-spoke stitch radiating from a center axis which can be used in circle, square, or diamond form. The circle version forms the nearest thing to a perfect circle that we can achieve in canvas embroidery. It is a charming rosette and is perfect for a decorative accent, a flower center, or when used in a group as a pattern. The Spider Web took care of the single isolated circles. This stitch is well named because it is a weaving process done on the surface of the canvas. It is secured to the canvas mesh only by the radiating spoke stitches and one stitch at the end of each encircling row.

The rhythmical scallop outline on the flowers is another decorative feature offering the chance to use ornamental stitches. In this case, there was an opportunity to make a nice ruffled edge, and there are two loop stitches, the Chain and the **Buttonhole,** which love to scoot around curves. I chose the Buttonhole, an old favorite of surface embroiderers which can easily be adapted to canvas embroidery. It was first used to bind the raveled edges of blankets and was thus known as the blanket stitch, and then used to bind the edges of buttonholes, when it became, not unnaturally, the Buttonhole stitch. The fluted area around

Algerian Eye, Spider Web, Fern

two of the flowers let me use two rows of encroaching Buttonhole stitches to make a handsome double-edge trim.

Now the spirit of the Jacobean design was starting to develop. There was lots going on. The buds and leaves called for leaf-shaped units. There was also a choice in this department. The Fern, the Cretan, and the Stem stitches all give nice texture as well as filling in oblong small shapes. I chose the Fern stitch because the leaves should be understated and there are no bold characteristics in this stitch. It is a full stitch, can conform

to any width or length desired, gives a nice texture, and its center stitches overlap, so there is no ridge running down the middle as there is in the others. A prominent center vein in this case would make the leaves too obvious.

The selection of these five stitches gave enough frosting to decorate the design in true Jacobean style. The ornamental stitches would lose their individuality if more were added, so the background and remaining sections of the flowers were done in our old standby, the **Tent** stitch.

ALGERIAN EYE

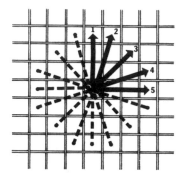

Starting from a center hole, make a wheel spoke, a vertical stitch covering 3 horizontal threads. Return needle to center. Number 2 stitch fans out to the same top level as the first stitch, only 1 thread to the right. Return needle to center. Number 3 stitch fans out covering only 2 horizontal threads, returning to center. Number 4 fans out over 3 horizontal threads, returning to center. Number 5 covers 3 horizontal threads making a true horizontal spoke. This completes the first quarter of the cartwheel. Continue these stitches in this sequence making a complete circuit to form the stitch. When these decorative stitch units are used as a pattern, the area around the circles is exposed, and a filler of a smaller eye stitch, cross-stitch, or Tent may be used.

The Square Algerian Eye is done in the same way except the spokes form a square rather than a circle. This stitch is often used for a border or is effective as a patterned background stitch. No compensating stitches or stitch units are needed when it is used as a grounding. In the square form, 5 spokes fan out to the same perimeter on all four sides from the center axle. This concentration of stitches completing the unit tends to make a rather bulky, large bump. If you want to flatten it, use thinner yarn.

The Diamond Eye, as one might suspect, is in the shape of a diamond when the unit is completed. Its center spoke covers 4 threads,

with each additional spoke of the quadrant also emanating from a center hole graduating on a true angle over 3 threads, 2, 3, and then 4 threads. It is effective as a decorative accent but it is particularly successful used as a patterned background. The outer edges of the units are squared and the spokes mesh symmetrically. There will be a slight exposure of canvas between the units when it is used as an allover pattern, but these threads are easily and effectively covered by a Back stitch.

FRENCH KNOT

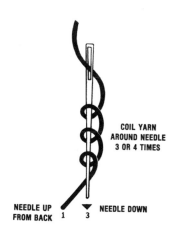

COIL YARN
AROUND NEEDLE
3 OR 4 TIMES

NEEDLE UP
FROM BACK   1   3   NEEDLE DOWN

These instructions may look formidable but this is a very old and popular stitch used for centuries by embroiderers in countries all over the world. One French Knot covers the space of one cross section or two holes of canvas. Bring the yarn up from the back of your work and coil it 2 to 4 times around the needle toward the point. The number of coils determines the size of the knot. Hold these coils fairly tightly with the working yarn in your left hand, and with this entire bundle of coils, insert the needle into the second hole in an erect bee-stinging fashion, pulling the needle out from the back of your work. Secure well. Heavy yarn is difficult to maneuver into a firm, consistent knot. A slim-eyed tapestry needle slips through the coils more easily.

SPIDER WEB

BUTTONHOLE

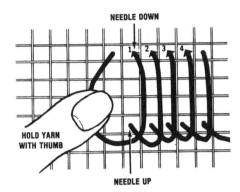

This is an elaborate stitch and looks far more difficult than it really is. It is really lots of fun, so don't let the directons frighten you.

Using a center hole for an axle, make an eight-spoked wheel covering 4 threads for each spoke. Working with a larger number of spokes tends to get confusing, unless you are weaving a web well over an inch in diameter. Bring the needle out 1 thread to the left and 1 thread *below* the center of a spoke. Without securing the yarn to the canvas, carry the yarn under this first spoke and spiral back over it, carrying the thread on to the next spoke. Spiral back over this one, too, and continue this procedure until you have completed the circle and all spokes are covered. Secure this first round by inserting the needle through the same hole in which you started the row. For the second round, again bring the yarn out 1 stitch below and to the left of the spoke. Go under the spoke, spiral back over it and on to the next spoke, and so forth. Repeat these rounds until the spokes are filled. You will see that a ridge forms over each spoke and a flat stitched area lies between the spokes. These webs are intricate little stitch units, charming as an accent where a circle is needed, but not recommended for repetitive pattern use as they are not substantially enough secured to the canvas to be durable.

This loop stitch can form either a trim straight binding or a fluted, curving piecrust edge. As a straight edge, it becomes an upright stitch and does not cover the canvas as well as when worked on an angle. There are, however, many ways to cover canvas, and one very attractive way is to make a double-edged trim of Buttonhole stitch as was done in the project. This is done in two operations. One set of stitches covers the outside edge, and then the canvas is turned around and the next set of stitches forms the inside or opposite edge. Use a 2-ply Persian yarn for the stitches of the outside edge of the area, and then when the canvas is turned around, use a single-ply yarn in a darker shade of the same color for the inner edge. Straddle the outside row of stitches with an encroaching inside row, making these stitches reach up to the rim of the outside row. This double edging can be worked on a straight line or around curves. Not only does it make a charming, far more interesting flounce, but it covers the canvas and softens the harshness of the outlining color, adding light to the outer rim and shadow and depth to the inner rim.

As with all loop stitches, the indispensable left thumb plays a major part. Begin rows or curves from left to right. Bring the needle out from the back of the canvas and pull yarn to the left with the left thumb. Insert the needle 1 thread over, and with the needle pointing down toward the bottom of the canvas, come out 4 threads directly below. Pass the needle over the yarn (this will be going through a loop). Insert the needle 4 threads up and 1 thread over, holding yarn to the left. Bring needle out below and through the loop. Continue this operation. A beaded-like piecrust edge formed by the loops will follow the outline of the design.

Left-handed workers should use the right thumb and begin rows from right to left.

down 1 thread over from top of left of second stitch and bring needle out. Insert needle 1 hole directly below base of this stitch #2 and come out 2 holes to the left and make this stitch match that of the opposite side. Continue this elongating as far as design prescribes. Though it is illustrated here as an object or stitch unit, an entire background may be made with this stitch by continuing the tracks straight down to the border. It makes a lovely striped effect and is beautiful when used with alternating colors. All rows should start at the top.

FERN

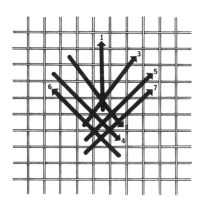

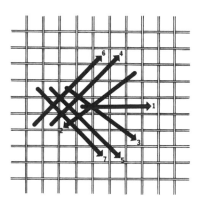

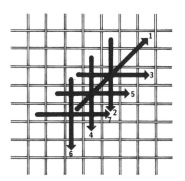

This stitch can be done vertically, horizontally, and diagonally. Its interlacing center makes a neat pattern and raises it from the canvas for an added accent.

To make a vertical leaf-shaped object, start at the top of the object and make a stitch over 4 horizontal threads. Bring the needle out 1 thread below and 2 threads to the left of the top of the first stitch, then insert it 3 vertical threads and 4 horizontal threads down to the right. Bring needle out 2 vertical threads to the left and insert it 3 vertical and 4 horizontal threads up to the right. This will match the stitch on the opposite side. Drop

To work the horizontal and diagonal Fern stitch, see diagrams.

Left-handed workers should start unit at bottom right and work to the left.

Index